THE
TOP 100
FINGER FOODS
FOR BABIES & TODDLERS

THE

TOP 100
FINGER FOODS
FOR BABIES & TODDLERS

Christine Bailey

DELICIOUS, HEALTHY MEALS FOR YOUR CHILD TO ENJOY

DUNCAN BAIRD PUBLISHERS

LONDON

The Top 100 Finger Foods For Babies & Toddlers
Christine Bailey

Distributed in the USA and Canada by
Sterling Publishing Co., Inc.
387 Park Avenue South
New York, NY 10016-8810

First published in the UK and USA in 2012 by
Duncan Baird Publishers Ltd
Sixth Floor, Castle House
75–76 Wells Street
London W1T 3QH

Managing Editor: Grace Cheetham
Editor: Alison Bolus
Managing Designer: Manisha Patel
Designer: Luana Gobbo
Commissioned Photography: Simon Smith
Food Stylist: Mari Williams
Prop Stylist: Lucy Harvey

Library of Congress Cataloging-in-Publication Data available

ISBN: 978-1-84899-015-9

10 9 8 7 6 5 4 3 2 1

Typeset in Helvetica
Color reproduction by Brightarts
Printed in China by Imago

For information about custom editions, special sales, premium
and corporate purchases, please contact Sterling Special Sales
Department at 800-805-5489 or specialsales@sterlingpub.com.

My sincere thanks go to Grace Cheetham for
commissioning me to write this great book. Thank you
also to my amazing editor, Alison Bolus, for all her
tireless patience, support and feedback. I would also
like to thank my wonderful husband, Chris, and my
three fantastic children, Nathan, Isaac and Simeon, for
tasting every recipe numerous times and providing me
with plenty of inspiration, love and support.

Publisher's Note
The information in this book is not intended as a substitute for
professional medical advice and treatment. If you are pregnant
or breastfeeding, or have any special dietary requirements or
medical conditions, it is recommended that you consult a
medical professional before following any of the information
or recipes contained in this book. Duncan Baird Publishers,
or any other persons who have been involved in working on
this publication, cannot accept responsibility for any errors
or omissions, inadvertent or not, that may be found in the
recipes or text, or for any problems that may arise as a result
of preparing one of these recipes or following the advice
contained in this work.

Notes on the Recipes
Unless otherwise stated:
Use large eggs
Use medium fruit and vegetables
Use fresh ingredients, including herbs and chilies
1 teaspoon = 5ml 1 tablespoon = 15ml 1 cup = 240ml

Symbols are used to identify even small amounts of an
ingredient. Where optional ingredients are listed, the symbols
reflect both ingredients, so a recipe using olive oil, with
coconut oil as an alternative, will not show the "nut-free"
symbol, in case the reader chooses the alternative. Dairy
foods may include cow, goat or sheep milk. Check the
manufacturer's labeling to ensure cheeses are vegetarian.
Give only the relevantly identified foods to those children with
a food allergy or intolerance.

contents

Key to symbols and Introduction   6

- CHAPTER ONE:
  BREAKFASTS   20

- CHAPTER TWO:
  LUNCHES   40

- CHAPTER THREE:
  SNACKS   70

- CHAPTER FOUR:
  DINNERS   88

- CHAPTER FIVE:
  DESSERTS   122

Menu Plans   140
Index   144

KEY TO SYMBOLS

Suitable for Vegetarians These recipes contain no meat, poultry, fish, seafood or animal byproducts, like gelatin.

Suitable for Vegans These recipes do not contain any meat, poultry, fish, seafood or other animal-derived ingredients, such as animal fats and gelatin. They also contain no eggs, dairy products or honey.

Gluten-free These recipes contain no gluten—a protein found in wheat, rye and barley as well as products containing these grains.

Wheat-free These recipes avoid any wheat grain or wheat-derived products—a common allergen.

Egg-free These recipes do not contain any egg or egg-based products.

Dairy-free These recipes do not include any dairy products, including cow milk, sheep milk and goat milk, and products derived from them.

Nut-free These recipes do not contain any nuts or nut-derived products. You may be able to replace nuts with seeds.

Seed-free These recipes do not contain any seeds, or their oils.

Soy-free These recipes do not contain soy or soy-based products, such as tofu, soy sauce, miso or soy milk.

Sugar-free In this book, the label "sugar-free" refers to food that is naturally sweetened with fruit only. I use xylitol as a sweetener in many recipes, but have classified it as a sugar.

INTRODUCTION

Every parent instinctively wants the best for their child. We want to help them grow up to be intelligent, happy and healthy, fully equipped to live their lives to the full. It is during childhood that they experience the most rapid growth and development, physically, mentally and emotionally. So if we're looking to maximize their potential, it is essential that we ensure that they are optimally nourished. The period between birth and five years is one of rapid growth and development, when children's energy demands soar as they become more independent. To fuel all of this activity, they need nutrient-dense foods in a form that will appeal to their little mouths and hands. This is where finger foods can be so important. By giving children a wide range of nutrient-dense bite-size foods, you can introduce them to new tastes and textures, encourage independent eating and nourish their active bodies.

ABOUT THIS BOOK

This book provides you with nutritional information on which foods to include in your child's diet, as well as featuring 100 delicious finger food recipes. The recipes are designed with preschoolers in mind, including many to tempt your little baby to start eating finger foods, but are equally suitable for older children and adults. Each recipe is packed with nutrients to optimize your child's growth and development, support immune health and provide essential nutrients for brain function. All the recipes are designed with our busy lifestyles in mind: Most are quick and easy to prepare. There are also recipes that are free from a variety of common allergens, and vegetarian and vegan options.

NUTRITIONAL NEEDS OF TODDLERS

Depending on their age, size and activity level, toddlers and preschoolers need around 1,000–1,400 calories each day. In addition to meeting their energy requirements, nutrient needs are particularly high as they reach various developmental milestones. Growth is an important physiological process during this age range, but, in addition, children's bodies are undergoing a number of changes internally. Their immune system is still relatively immature, and organs such as lungs and the digestive system are still developing. The brain is growing at a rapid rate. In fact, the brain increases in size by around 50% between the ages of one and five years. In addition, however, toddlers have made the transition from being fed to feeding themselves. This is a crucial time when they start to develop preferences and attitudes about food that can greatly influence the quality of the food they eat and the nutrients they receive.

In view of their small size, preschool children can find it difficult to eat sufficient amounts of food at any one time to fulfill their high nutritional needs, so all meals and snacks should be nutrient-dense.

THE ESSENTIAL BUILDING BLOCKS

During children's early years and beyond, it is important to ensure their diet is varied and contains all the key elements for growth and development. Below are the essential components for a healthy diet.

Protein

Protein provides amino acids, the building blocks of the body. These are vital for the development of the skeletal structure, including bones, cartilage, ligaments, teeth and nails, as well as for the body's hormonal system, development of new muscle, organ tissue and neurotransmitters—the chemical messengers of the brain. Deficiency in amino acids can therefore influence growth and development as well as affect mood, behavior, memory and concentration.

The quality of a protein is determined by its balance of amino acids. Though there are 23 amino acids from which the body can build everything, only eight are considered essential because these can come only through the diet, while the others can be made by the body. All animal products (meat, dairy, eggs, fish, seafood) provide these eight amino acids, whereas vegetables sources (with the exception of foods such as soy, quinoa and green superfoods, for example chlorella and spirulina) are incomplete. Therefore, with a vegetarian diet it is necessary to include a wide range of different vegetable sources in the daily diet.

Protein requirements are calculated on body weight, with adjustments made as children grow older. Healthy one- to three-year-old children need 0.55 grams of protein per pound of body weight each day, which means that for a child weighing 29 pounds the requirement is 16 grams of protein per day. To ensure sufficient protein, your child needs to eat two to three servings of protein a day. As a general guide, an ounce of meat or fish provides around 7g protein. A serving size looks like 2 to 4 tablespoons of grated cheese, 1 egg, 2 tablespoons of fish or meat, or 2 to 5 tablespoons of beans.

Carbohydrates

To fuel their rapid growth and development, children need adequate amounts of carbohydrate. Carbohydrate-rich foods, such as fruits, vegetables, bread, pasta and rice, are broken down into glucose during digestion. The glucose is then absorbed into the bloodstream. For sustained energy, it is vital that the supply of glucose remains even throughout the day. Refined carbohydrates and sugary foods, such as white bread and rice, cookies, cakes and sugary drinks, are broken down quickly by the body, causing a rapid rise in blood sugar levels. This results in insulin being released, and the resulting dip in blood sugar will cause your child to feel irritable and moody, to lack concentration and crave more sugar. The result is see-sawing blood sugar levels.

To ensure more balanced blood sugar levels, choose carbohydrates that release glucose slowly into the bloodstream, such as vegetables, beans and lentils, fresh fruit and whole grains. You can also use something called the Glycemic Load (GL). This measures the effect of a food on blood glucose levels. Foods with a low score (below 10) should form the main carbohydrates in your child's diet, and foods with scores of 11 to 14 be eaten in moderation. Examples of moderate and low GL foods include whole grains, oats, vegetables, beans and lentils, and fruits such as berries, plums, pears, apples and citrus fruits. One way to keep a meal balanced is to include some protein or healthy fat with a carbohydrate food, because this can slow down how quickly glucose is released. For example, a slice of wholegrain toast with nut butter is a better option than a slice of wholegrain toast with honey. Although whole grains are nutritious, too many can fill a child up too quickly without providing sufficient calories or nutrients for their needs. As their digestive systems are still immature, too many grains can cause digestive upsets as well as being potential allergens. It is healthier to focus more on nutrient-rich vegetables, which are gentler on the digestive system. While some fruits are faster-releasing than others, eating whole fresh fruit is better than drinking fruit juice. Whole fruits provide soluble fiber, which slows down the release of sugars found in the fruit. Fruits are also rich in vitamins, minerals and antioxidants, which are important for your child's health. Dried fruit (a concentrated source of sugar) should be eaten only in small quantities.

Portion Size Ranges

Toddler appetites vary from meal to meal and day to day, so a portion size range is generally recommended. Sometimes toddlers eat very small portions of food, especially if they are tired or unwell. At other times they may eat larger portions, for example after a lot of active play. Offering a nutrient-rich diet and allowing toddlers to eat to their appetite is the best strategy. Each day aim for your toddler to be eating at least two pieces of fruit plus four servings of vegetables. A serving is ½ to 1 piece of fruit, such as an apple or tangerine, and ½ to 1 tablespoon vegetables or around four florets (e.g. broccoli). For grains, a serving is around 2 to 5 tablespoons cooked pasta or rice, ½ to 1 slice of bread, or 1 to 3 tablespoons mashed potato, with around half of this being whole grains. When planning a meal, aim for half their plate to be full of vegetables, one-fourth protein-rich foods and the remaining fourth starchy carbohydrates, such as pasta or grains.

Essential Fats

Fat gets a lot of bad press, but the truth is that the right types of fats are essential for your child's health. Fat plays an important role in the provision of energy as well as being crucial for the maturation of organs, immune function and building a healthy brain. But your child needs the right kind of fat in the right quantities.

Essential fats—the omega-3 and omega-6 fatty acids (polyunsaturated fats)—are particularly important for the development of the brain and body systems, including the nervous system, hormonal system and digestive tract. Insufficiency in these fats can lead to dry, flaky skin, dry hair and dandruff, and itchy eyes as well as poor memory, short attention span, mood swings and concentration problems. The other types of fats include saturated fats, monounsaturated fats and cholesterol. These fats can be made by the body, unlike the essential omega fats, which have to be supplied through the diet. Therefore, focus on providing sufficient omega fats in your child's diet and in particular omega-3 fats, which are often deficient in children's diets.

The omega-3 parent fatty acid is known as alpha-linolenic acid (ALA) and is converted by the body into the metabolically active EPA (eicosapentaenoic acid) and DHA (docosahexaenoic acid). However, this conversion is inefficient, so it is important to include foods that provide a direct source of EPA and DHA, such as oily fish (for example, salmon, sardines, mackerel, herring, trout, halibut, anchovies). One caution however: larger oily fish, such as shark, tend to be higher in heavy metals like mercury and pesticides than small oily fish, and so are best avoided. Canned tuna is also not a good source of omega-3 fats, because the canning process removes most of them. The omega-3 content of farmed fish depends on the quality of their diet, so, where possible, opt for wild, sustainably caught oily fish, such as Alaskan salmon, or organic farmed fish.

Another souce of omega-3 fats is seeds such as flaxseed, hemp seed or pumpkin seeds. But since the conversion process of ALA to EPA and DHA from seeds is inefficient, a supplement may be appropriate for vegetarians (see page 18).

Fat provides a useful source of energy in a child's diet, so it is recommended that around 30% of their total calorie intake should be fat, with no more than one-third saturated fat and at least one-third essential fats. Damaged or hydrogenated fats found in processed or fried foods and some margarines are harmful for health and so should not figure in your child's diet. A lowfat diet is also not recommended for young children, because it will not provide them with sufficient calories and can be lower in valuable fat-soluble vitamins, such as vitamin D. It is recommended that children under one year should drink breast or formula milk, with organic whole cow's milk or alternatives for recipes. milk. Organic whole milk is recommended for children between one and two years of age; you can switch to lower fat (1% or 2%) milk after age two.

To ensure the presence of sufficient omega fats, aim for your child to eat fish two times a week, focusing on oily fish, and include seeds or seed oils daily. Seed oils such as flaxseed and hemp seed are readily available and can be useful for adding to dressings, dips and spreads or poured over warm foods, but must not be heated. Other good sources include walnuts, chia seeds, pumpkin seeds, tofu, leafy green vegetables, such as broccoli and kale, and organic or omega-3-rich eggs.

Careful choices need to be made when cooking with oils. While omega-3 and -6 fats are essential for your child's health, they are also prone to damage by cooking, heating and food processing and are therefore not suitable as a cooking oil. The best oil you can use is organic coconut oil, which is less prone to damage on heating.

Olive oil is primarily a monounsaturated fat. While inherently more stable than a polyunsaturated fat (for example omega-3 and -6 oils), it is still vulnerable when heated. However, since it can be beneficial for health, you can use it in dressings and when cooking at low temperatures. Polyunsaturated oils (for example vegetable oils such as corn, soy and sunflower) are not recommended because they will rapidly form trans-fats when heated.

Vitamins and Minerals

The entire range of vitamins and minerals is essential for the growth and health of your toddler, because toddlers have high nutrient demands and generally low stores of these micronutrients.

However, national dietary surveys highlight the often limited range of foods eaten by toddlers, making them vulnerable to vitamin and mineral deficiencies. A range of vitamins and minerals, for example, are required for brain function, including B vitamins, folic acid, vitamin C, magnesium, manganese and zinc. The B vitamins are particularly important because the brain uses vast amounts of them. Good

sources include whole grains, leafy green vegetables, lean meat, fish and eggs.

Antioxidants are important to help protect your child's brain and body from harmful oxidants known as free radicals. These can damage your child's cells and tissues, affecting the function and health of body systems and impairing immune function. Constant exposure to free radicals in our environment, fried and processed foods and additives means that your child's requirements for antioxidants on a daily basis are high. Key antioxidants include beta-carotene, vitamin C, vitamin E, selenium, glutathione, coenzyme Q10 and phytonutrients—plant compounds present in fresh fruits and vegetables. One of the best ways to ensure a good daily intake is to include a colorful selection of fruits and vegetables.

Vitamin D plays an important role in many body systems, including bone health and immune function. However, vitamin

D deficiency is increasingly common in children. The main source of vitamin D is sunlight. Food sources are limited and include fortified foods, eggs and oily fish. A vitamin D supplement of 400ius daily may be appropriate for both infants and older children.

Calcium and magnesium are also essential for bone health, and toddlers require around 700mg calcium and 80–130mg magnesium daily. A serving of 8 ounces plain lowfat yogurt contains 415mg calcium and 1 cup lowfat (2%) milk contains 293mg. So two to three servings a day of calcium-rich foods are sufficient to meet requirements. Other useful sources of calcium include canned fish, tofu, almonds, tahini and leafy vegetables.

Iron deficiency can be a common problem in young children. Too little iron can slow their growth, lead to low energy levels and increase susceptibility to infection. Iron is also vital for the developing brain and cognitive function. Good iron-rich foods include leafy green vegetables, lean meats, eggs, beans and lentils, dried fruit, and fortified wholegrain cereals. Try to ensure that your toddler eats iron-rich foods daily.

Drinks

The best drink for your child in between meals is water. Avoid sweetened colas and other fizzy drinks, juice drinks with added sugar, and flavored milks, which are often high in additives and sweeteners. If giving fruit juice, dilute it at least half and half with water. If your child has had diarrhea, coconut water is a good drink, as it is rich in potassium, magnesium and calcium, making it an effective rehydrating drink at times. It can also help prevent constipation.

FOODS TO AVOID

In addition to including nutrient-rich foods, it is important to steer clear of foods that contain a lot of sugar, salt and food additives. Opt for minimally processed foods whenever possible.

No to Sugar

Both refined sugar and processed carbohydrates are devoid of nutrients and lead to blood sugar imbalances. For this reason, I've suggested in this book that you use xylitol. With a low glycemic index, xylitol has minimal impact on blood glucose levels and may help to maintain healthy teeth. If you cannot find xylitol, use raw cane sugar instead. Honey should not be given to children under one year.

Be careful of foods and drinks labeled "sugar-free" as these will often contain aspartame and saccharin, which may adversely affect your child's behavior.

Go Low with Salt

Unfortunately, many processed foods, including those that are aimed at toddlers, can be high in salt. These include foods such as breads, cereals, snack foods, cookies and processed meats and cheese. Toddlers should consume only 2g salt a day; for babies this is only 1g.

Keep Your Child Chemical-Free

Food colorings, flavorings, preservatives and pesticides can all adversely affect your child's health and behavior. Some of these are natural ingredients and harmless, but it is best to steer clear of any product with a long list of chemical-sounding names. Many of these chemicals are antinutrients —substances that interfere with our ability to absorb or to use essential nutrients and can also promote the loss of important nutrients from the body.

CATERING FOR DIETS AND ALLERGIES

Allergies to certain foods are increasingly common, particularly in young children. Allergies can cause a diverse range of symptoms including fatigue, irritability, behavioral problems, hyperactivity and digestive upsets. Immune-system reactions can involve IgE antibodies resulting in an immediate, severe and potentially life-threatening reaction or more delayed IgG reactions, which can take anywhere from an hour to three days to show themselves. Food intolerances and sensitivities are reactions to food where there is no measurable antibody response. This can include lactose intolerance, where a child lacks the enzyme to digest milk sugar (lactose) and can develop diarrhea and abdominal pain. The most common allergens are wheat and other gluten grains, milk, eggs, yeast-containing foods, shellfish, nuts, peanuts and soy.

The recipes in this book are clearly labeled for many of these key allergens, and many of the recipes are gluten-free and dairy-free. In addition, you can easily alter many of the recipes, for example using tamari soy sauce instead of standard soy sauce to make them gluten-free. If you think your child is reacting to certain foods, it is worth seeking the advice of a qualified nutritionist to help with testing and devising an alternative nutrient-rich diet. Digestive problems are often the underlying factor in IgG allergies, so it is important to heal the gut with supplements as well as removing aggravating foods. Seek the support of a nutritional therapist.

If there is a family history of allergies (including eczema, asthma and hay fever), introduce new foods, particularly the common allergenic foods, one at a time and watch for any reaction.

Vegetarian Toddlers

A vegetarian diet for a toddler requires careful consideration and planning to ensure they receive all the nutrients they need to thrive. Certain nutrients can be low in vegetarian diets, including protein, essential fats, iron, zinc, calcium, iodine, vitamin B12 and vitamin D. Make sure you include plenty of nutrient-dense foods, such as dairy foods, avocados, eggs, ground nuts and seeds, nut and seed oils and nut butters (as long as there is no family history of allergies). Also, make sure that their diet is not too high in fiber-rich foods, which can upset their digestion and fill them up so that they do not receive adequate calories and energy.

SUPPLEMENTS

Nutrient deficiencies in children are quite common. Include a children's multivitamin and mineral formula in your child's diet as a useful insurance to keep your child physically and mentally healthy. Choose one free from added sugars, sweeteners, artificial flavors and colorings.

Many children are low in the essential omegas, so it is worth considering a supplement. Look for those that contain omega-3 fats DHA and EPA and the omega-6 fat GLA (gamma linolenic acid), found in evening primrose and borage oils.

You may also wish to give your toddler a probiotic, especially after a stomach bug, diarrhea or being on a course of antibiotics. Probiotics are beneficial bacteria in the gut that maintain a healthy digestive system and support immune health.

SAFETY WITH FINGER FOODS

While finger foods are a great way to encourage independent eating, there is a slight risk of choking. Make sure your child sits down while he eats, and never leave him alone during meals. Teach him to chew and swallow before talking. Cut grapes and other fruits, meat, cheese and raw vegetables into small pieces that won't block airways.

Offer plenty of liquids to children when eating, but make sure liquids and solids are not swallowed at the same time.

VITAMIN / MINERAL	KEY FOOD SOURCES	SIGNS OF DEFICIENCY
B Vitamins Needed for energy production, important for function of the heart, nervous system	Whole grains, leafy green vegetables, eggs, meat, fish, beans and lentils	Low energy, depression, poor concentration and focus
Calcium Necessary for growth and maintenance of strong bones, teeth and cell walls, needed to regulate muscle contraction and heartbeat	Dairy products, nuts, seeds, leafy green vegetables, canned fish with bones, dried fruit, fortified milk	Anxiety, insomnia, poor bone and teeth health
Vitamin D Processed into a hormone via the liver and kidneys, it regulates calcium absorption—important for cell division and immune function	Main source is sunlight, plus oily fish, fortified dairy products, shiitake mushrooms and eggs	Low immune function, depression, poor bone and teeth health
Zinc Vital component of many enzymes and necessary for energy production, wound healing and cell production	Seafood, nuts, seeds, plain yogurt, tahini, eggs, lean meats	Low immune function, poor appetite, loss of taste and smell, lack of concentration, slow wound healing
Iron Necessary for the production of hemoglobin in red blood cells and transporting oxygen around the body; needed for many of the body's enzymes	Leafy green vegetables, lean meats, eggs, beans and lentils, fortified cereals	Low energy, pallor, weakness, poor concentration, low immune function, depression, poor cognitive function, spoon-shaped nails or with ridges running lengthwise
Magnesium Vital for the function of enzymes for energy production, cell metabolism, muscle and nerve function	Leafy green vegetables, nuts, seeds, beans and lentils	Irritability, anxiety, muscle cramps, low energy, poor bone and teeth health, depression, insomnia

BREAKFASTS

To get your child off to the best start in the day, breakfast is vital. Even if you feel rushed in the mornings or your child has a limited appetite, there are plenty of options in this chapter to suit the fussiest of eaters. If you provide them with a nourishing, low glycemic breakfast, children will have more stable energy levels to help them concentrate through the morning. All the recipes in this chapter focus on slow-releasing carbohydrates, fiber, protein and essential fats to provide everything your child needs to make the most of their day ahead. Whether it is some Tropical Breakfast Bars or Cheesy-Chili Muffins, these finger foods are ideal to nourish the whole family—simple and fuss-free, making it easy to experience a healthier start to the day.

cranberry-seed bread

MAKES 1 LOAF (10 SLICES)

PREPARATION + COOKING
15 + 40 minutes

STORAGE
Keep in the fridge for 2 to 3 days or freeze for up to 1 month.

SERVE THIS WITH...
Almond-Chocolate Butter (see p.73) or pure fruit spread

HEALTH BENEFITS
Pumpkin seeds are nutrient-dense nuggets for children, providing plenty of protein and essential omega-3 and -6 fats as well as bone-supporting minerals manganese, magnesium, phosphorous and zinc. They are perfect for boosting flagging energy levels, being rich in protein and energy-giving nutrients iron, copper, zinc, magnesium and B vitamins.

A delicious quick and easy sweet bread packed with omega-rich seeds and fiber. Using frozen cranberries keeps the bread beautifully moist.

light olive oil, for greasing
1½ cups self-rising wholewheat flour
1 teaspoon baking soda
2 tablespoons pumpkin seeds
2 tablespoons sunflower seeds
2 tablespoons sesame seeds
5 eggs

½ cup raw cane sugar or xylitol
finely grated zest of 1 orange
1 tablespoon vanilla extract
⅓ cup olive oil or melted coconut oil
heaped 1 cup frozen cranberries

1 Preheat the oven to 350°F. Lightly grease a loaf pan (about 8 x 4 x 2½ inch) and line it with parchment paper.

2 Put the flour, baking soda and seeds in a large bowl and stir well to mix.

3 In another bowl, beat together the eggs, sugar, orange zest and vanilla until light and fluffy. Add the beaten mixture and the olive oil to the dry ingredients and mix well. Stir in the cranberries.

4 Pour the batter into the pan and bake until golden brown and firm to the touch, 35 to 40 minutes.

5 Let cool in the pan a little before unmolding. Cut into slices to serve while still warm, or serve toasted.

carrot & raisin buns

These fiber-rich sweet buns resemble little carrot cakes, but are much healthier.

scant ½ cup light olive oil, plus extra for greasing
3 eggs, beaten
heaped ¾ cup self-rising wholewheat flour
scant 1 cup self-rising white flour
pinch of ground cinnamon
2 carrots, peeled and finely shredded
¼ cup raisins
2 tablespoons dried shredded coconut
scant ½ cup canned crushed pineapple, drained

1 Preheat the oven to 350°F. Lightly grease 10 cups in a mini muffin pan (gem pan).
2 Beat together the oil and eggs to form a thick emulsion. Sift the flours into a bowl and add the cinnamon, carrots, raisins and coconut. Stir in the oil mixture and pineapple.
3 Spoon the batter into the prepared muffin cups.
4 Bake until firm and golden, about 20 minutes. Let cool in the muffin pan 5 minutes, then unmold onto a wire rack to cool completely.

MAKES 10

PREPARATION + COOKING
15 + 20 minutes

STORAGE
Keep in the fridge for 2 to 3 days or freeze for up to 1 month.

SERVE THIS WITH...
scrambled or boiled egg

HEALTH BENEFITS
Carrots are one of the richest sources of carotenoids: antioxidants known to promote healthy eyesight and protect the skin and eyes from UV damage. Carrots are easy to digest, even for babies, and, being rich in soluble fiber, help to promote healthy bowel function and regulate blood sugar levels.

Ⓥ Ⓧ Ⓧ ⊘ ⊘ ⊘ ⊘

date & spice muffins

MAKES 6

These tasty muffins are gluten- and dairy-free.

PREPARATION + COOKING
15 + 20 minutes

STORAGE
Keep in the fridge for 2 to 3 days
or freeze for up to 1 month.

SERVE THIS WITH...
fresh fruit
yogurt smoothie

HEALTH BENEFITS
Cinnamon is a wonderful,
warming spice known to help
stabilize blood sugar levels by
improving the uptake of glucose
into the cells. It also lowers
inflammation in the body and
appears to possess antibacterial
and antifungal properties,
making it useful against bacterial
and yeast infections.

4 tablespoons light olive oil,
    plus extra for greasing
½ cup almonds
½ cup coconut flour
½ cup gluten-free
    all-purpose flour
½ teaspoon baking soda
pinch of salt
2 teaspoons gluten-free baking
    powder
1 teaspoon ground cinnamon
⅓ cup minced pitted dates

2 tablespoons raw cane sugar
    or xylitol
2 bananas
4 eggs

CRUMBLE TOPPING
2 tablespoons gluten-free oats
    or buckwheat flakes
1 tablespoon raw cane sugar
    or xylitol
1 teaspoon ground cinnamon
1 tablespoon light olive oil

1 Preheat the oven to 350°F. Grease a 6-cup muffin pan.

2 Pulse the topping ingredients in a food processor.

3 Put the almonds in a blender and blend to form a flour.
Tip into a bowl and add the coconut flour, gluten-free
flour, baking soda, baking powder, salt and cinnamon.
Stir in the dates.

4 Blend together the oil, sugar, bananas and eggs.
Pour into the almond mixture and beat for 5 minutes.

5 Spoon the batter into the prepared muffin pan and
sprinkle on the topping. Bake until firm and golden,
15 to 20 minutes. Let cool completely in the muffin pan.

crunchy granola bites

Delicious crunchy oats, nuts and seeds are coated with a naturally sweet date paste and baked to form crisp nuggets.

light olive oil, for greasing
1½ cups rolled oats
⅔ cup sliced almonds
½ cup chopped pecans
3 tablespoons flaked
    unsweetened coconut
½ cup mixed dried berries
¼ cup sunflower seeds
2 tablespoons sesame seeds
½ teaspoon ground cinnamon
⅓ cup olive oil or melted
    coconut oil
⅓ cup pitted dates
½ teaspoon vanilla extract

1 Preheat the oven to 300°F. Lightly grease a baking sheet and line it with parchment paper.

2 Put the oats, nuts, coconut, berries, seeds and cinnamon in a large bowl and toss well.

3 Pour the olive oil into a blender. Add the dates and vanilla extract and blend to form a sticky paste. Stir the mixture into the oats and mix thoroughly until everything is slightly sticky. Squeeze the mixture into little walnut-size "nuggets" and space them out evenly on the prepared baking sheet.

4 Bake until golden brown, about 45 minutes. Let cool on the baking sheet.

SERVES 6

PREPARATION + COOKING
10 + 45 minutes

STORAGE
Keep in an airtight container for 1 to 2 weeks.

SERVE THIS WITH...
fresh fruit

HEALTH BENEFITS
Oats are a perfect breakfast food for young children, providing plenty of slow-releasing carbohydrate and fiber to keep blood sugar levels even through the morning. They are a good source of the mineral magnesium, which is essential for energy production yet is often lacking in children's diet. Oats also provide selenium—an important antioxidant that protects the body from damage.

tropical breakfast bars

HEALTH BENEFITS
If your child seems in low spirits and lethargic, cashew nuts may be the perfect food. Rich in copper and iron, cashew nuts can help to build red blood cells, which are essential for maintaining energy and brain function. They are also a useful source of the mineral magnesium (important for bone health) plus zinc to keep the immune system functioning optimally.

The delicious combination of pineapple and cashew nuts makes these the perfect "grab and go" healthy breakfast bars when time is short. Adding nut butter to the flour mixture greatly increases the protein and minerals in this bar and will help to satisfy even the hungriest of toddlers.

scant ¼ cup light olive oil,
plus extra for greasing
1½ cups dried pineapple
pieces, chopped
¼ ripe pineapple, flesh diced
heaped ⅓ cup cashew nut
butter or other nut butter

1¾ cups rolled oats
scant 1¼ cups self-rising
wholewheat flour
1 teaspoon baking powder
2 tablespoons ground flaxseed
2 tablespoons sesame seeds
1 cup dried shredded coconut

MAKES 16

PREPARATION + COOKING
20 + 35 minutes

STORAGE
Keep in the fridge for 1 week
or freeze for up to 1 month.

SERVE THIS WITH...
fresh fruit

1 Preheat the oven to 350°F. Lightly grease a 10- x 12-inch shallow baking pan and line it with parchment paper.

2 Put the dried pineapple pieces in a bowl and cover with boiling water. Let soak for 15 minutes, then drain.

3 Put half of the dried pineapple into a blender with the fresh pineapple, cashew nut butter and oil, and blend to form a thick purée.

4 Put the oats, flour and baking powder in a bowl. Stir in the seeds, coconut and remaining dried pineapple. Pour in the purée and mix thoroughly.

5 Spoon into the prepared pan and bake until golden brown, 30 to 35 minutes. Let cool in the pan before cutting into 16 bars.

MAKES 12

raisin-quinoa slices

PREPARATION + COOKING
15 + 40 minutes

Quinoa flakes are a nutrient-rich gluten-free addition to these bars and easy to digest, making them a perfect food for young children.

STORAGE
Keep in the fridge for 2 to 3 days, or slice and freeze for up to 1 month.

SERVE THIS WITH...
Greek yogurt
fresh fruit or a vegetable juice

HEALTH BENEFITS
Energizing and nutritious buckwheat is a delicious gluten-free grain particularly rich in magnesium—a critical mineral for supporting energy production in the body. It is a rich source of flavonoids (especially rutin), which are potent antioxidants shown to improve blood flow and circulation. It is a good source of fiber, too, helping to nourish the digestive system and keeping energy levels stable through the day.

light olive oil, for greasing
2 apples, peeled and grated
⅓ cup rice flour
½ cup buckwheat flour
heaped ⅓ cup quinoa flakes
2 tablespoons raw cacao powder or 1 tablespoon unsweetened cocoa powder
½ teaspoon ground cinnamon
2 teaspoons gluten-free baking powder

1 tablespoon ground flaxseed
⅓ cup olive oil or melted coconut oil
2 tablespoons raw cane sugar or xylitol
½ cup raisins
2 tablespoons mixed seeds, such as sunflower and sesame
2 eggs, beaten

1 Preheat the oven to 350°F. Lightly grease an 8-inch square baking pan.

2 Put the apples, flours, quinoa flakes, cacao powder, cinnamon, baking powder and flaxseed in a mixing bowl.

3 Heat the oil with the sugar in a small pan, then add to the flour along with the raisins, seeds and eggs and mix thoroughly together.

4 Spoon the batter into the prepared pan and bake until golden brown, about 40 minutes. Cut into bars while warm, then let cool in the pan.

berry blinis with sweet cherry sauce

These tasty pancakes are packed with protein.

1 cup self-rising wholewheat
  flour
¾ cup buckwheat flour
2 teaspoons baking powder
2 eggs, separated
generous ¾ cup lowfat mil
scant 1 cup ricotta cheese
¾ cup frozen mixed berries

1 tablespoon olive oil or melted
  coconut oil

CHERRY SAUCE
½ cup fresh or thawed frozen
  pitted cherries
1 tablespoon raw cane sugar
  or xylitol

SERVES 4

PREPARATION + COOKING
15 + 14 minutes

STORAGE
Keep the blinis in the fridge
for 1 to 2 days and the sauce for
2 to 3 days.

SERVE THIS WITH...
toasted pistachio nuts
plain yogurt

HEALTH BENEFITS
Like all berries, cherries are
exceptionally rich in antioxidants,
especially anthocyanidins, which
can help to prevent or repair
cell damage from free radicals.
These antioxidants can also
help lower inflammation in the
body, which may help with skin
conditions such as eczema.
Being a low glycemic index fruit,
they make an ideal snack for
babies and toddlers to balance
blood sugar levels through the
morning.

1 To make the cherry sauce, put the cherries and sugar in a food processor and blitz to form a thick sauce.
2 Mix together the flours and baking powder in a bowl. Make a well in the center and gradually beat in the egg yolks, milk and ricotta. Beat thoroughly. Stir in the berries.
3 Beat the egg whites until stiff. Stir a spoonful into the ricotta mixture to loosen, then fold in the rest.
4 Heat a little oil in a frying pan. Put 4 tablespoons of batter into the pan to form 4 little pancakes. Cook until little bubbles appear on the surface, about 2 minutes, then flip the blinis over and cook until the other side is golden, about 1 minute. Cover while making 4 more blinis.
5 Serve the blinis with the cherry sauce drizzled over.

almond & apricot pancakes

These gluten-free pancakes are sweetened with apricots and use almonds instead of flour.

MAKES 12 (SERVES 4 TO 6)

PREPARATION + COOKING
20 + 15 minutes + soaking + resting

STORAGE
Keep in the fridge for 1 to 2 days.

SERVE THIS WITH...
chopped pitted apricots
Greek yogurt

HEALTH BENEFITS
Toddlers can often have low iron levels, resulting in flagging energy, poor concentration and susceptibility to infections. Dried apricots are a useful vegetarian source of iron, providing 6.3mg iron per 100g. They are also a concentrated source of other minerals, including potassium, as well as the bone-friendly nutrients calcium, magnesium and beta-carotene.

¼ cup moist dried apricots, chopped
juice of 1 orange
1⅓ cups almonds
2 eggs
1 tablespoon light olive oil
2 teaspoons vanilla extract
½ teaspoon baking soda
1 teaspoon gluten-free baking powder
2 tablespoons olive oil

1 Soak the apricots in the juice for 10 minutes to soften.

2 Put the almonds in a blender and blend to form a flour. Tip into a bowl and set aside.

3 Put the apricots and juice, eggs, oil and vanilla in the blender and blend until smooth. Add the almond flour, baking soda and baking powder and blend to form a smooth batter. Let rest for 10 minutes.

4 Heat a little oil in a large frying pan. Put 4 large spoonfuls of the batter into the pan to make 4 pancakes. Cook until bubbles form on the surface, 2 to 3 minutes. Flip the pancakes over and cook until golden, about 2 minutes. Remove from the pan and cover to keep warm while you make the remaining pancakes. Serve hot.

apple-cinnamon french toast

Give French toast a fruity twist with these delicious bite-size toasted sandwiches. Choose wholewheat bread for slow-releasing carbohydrates and additional fiber.

2 apples, peeled, cored and
    chopped
1 teaspoon ground cinnamon
4 slices of wholewheat bread

2 eggs
4 tablespoons lowfat (2%) milk
1 tablespoon olive oil or melted
    coconut oil

1 Put the apples in a small pan with 2 tablespoons water. Cover and simmer until soft, about 10 minutes. Purée with a hand blender or press through a strainer. Let cool, then stir in half of the cinnamon.

2 Spread 2 slices of bread with the apple purée. Put the other slices on top to form 2 sandwiches.

3 Combine the eggs, milk and remaining cinnamon in a bowl and whisk well. Heat the oil in a large frying pan.

4 Carefully dip the sandwiches into the egg mixture to coat all over. Put the sandwiches in the pan and fry gently until golden, 3 to 4 minutes per side.

5 Remove from the pan and let cool slightly, then cut into quarters and serve.

SERVES 1

PREPARATION + COOKING
15 + 14 minutes

STORAGE
Best eaten immediately.

SERVE THIS WITH...
Greek or plain yogurt

HEALTH BENEFITS
Apples contain plant compounds called polyphenols, which have been shown to support immune health and lower inflammation in the body. Being rich in soluble fiber and pectin, they are particularly useful for tackling stomach troubles and improving bowel health. Keeping the skin on some of the apples will provide additional fiber and nutrients.

chocolate-peanut waffles

MAKES 8

PREPARATION + COOKING
15 + 10 minutes

STORAGE
Keep in the fridge for 1 day.

SERVE THIS WITH...
fresh fruit
yogurt
Sweet Cherry Sauce
  (see page 29)

Quick and easy to make, and packed with energizing protein and slow-releasing carbs, this sensational breakfast treat will be a firm family favorite. The waffles are delicious served with fresh fruit and yogurt, but are also wonderful served plain as a snack at any time of day.

HEALTH BENEFITS
Chocolate can be a healthy food as long as you use it in its low-processed unsweetened, bittersweet or semi-sweet form. Dark chocolate, raw chocolate, cocoa and raw cacao powder are rich in flavonoids —powerful antioxidants known to help protect the body from damage. They also contain brain-stimulating chemicals such as theobromine, tyramine and phenylethylamine, which can lift mood and boost brain function.

¾ cup self-rising wholewheat
  flour
½ cup all-purpose white flour
1 teaspoon baking powder
2 tablespoons unsweetened
  cocoa powder
2 eggs

3 tablespoons natural
  peanut butter
2 tablespoons raw cane sugar
  or xylitol
1 tablespoon light olive oil,
  plus extra for greasing
¾ cup whole or lowfat (2%) milk

1 Sift the flours, baking powder and cocoa powder into a food processor, tipping in the bran from the sifter.

2 Put the eggs, peanut butter, sugar and oil in a bowl and whisk to combine. Add to the processor and blitz with enough of the milk to form a thick batter.

3 Grease a waffle iron and ladle some of the batter onto it, according to the manufacturer's directions. Cook until the waffles are golden and crisp, 4 to 5 minutes. Repeat with the remaining batter.

4 Serve the waffles hot or cold.

fruity popovers

Children love these fruit-filled batter puffs.

heaped ¾ cup all-purpose flour,
    sifted
1 tablespoon ground flaxseed
2 tablespoons raw cane sugar
    or xylitol
4 eggs

1¼ cups whole or lowfat (2%)
    milk
2 ripe pears, peeled, cored
    and diced
1 large handful of blueberries
1 tablespoon olive oil

SERVES 4

PREPARATION + COOKING
10 + 25 minutes + chilling

STORAGE
Keep in the fridge for 1 day.

SERVE THIS WITH...
poached or fresh berries
plain yogurt

1 Put the flour, flaxseed and sugar in a bowl. Whisk in the eggs, then pour in the milk slowly while whisking, to avoid lumps. Cover the bowl with plastic wrap and leave overnight in the fridge.
2 Preheat the oven to 425°F. Spoon the fruit into the batter mixture and stir to combine.
3 Put a little oil into 4 cups in a muffin pan and heat in the oven until hot, about 5 minutes. Remove from the oven and quickly fill the cups with the fruit batter.
4 Bake until puffed and golden brown, 20 to 25 minutes.
5 Let cool slightly before serving.

HEALTH BENEFITS
To keep energy levels high in the morning, opt for fruits with a low glycemic index, such as pears. A good source of soluble fiber, they are also a low-allergen fruit, making them a perfect choice for young children. Pears are also a good source of potassium, to help balance fluid levels, rehydrate the body following bouts of diarrhea and prevent muscle cramp. Flaxseed will increase the fiber content and omega-3 fats, too.

vegetable rostis with herbed cottage cheese

SERVES 4

PREPARATION + COOKING
15 + 10 minutes

STORAGE
Keep in the fridge for 2 days.

SERVE THIS WITH...
baked beans
broiled tomatoes

HEALTH BENEFITS
Parsley is an incredibly nutritious herb, rich in iron and vitamin C, making it a wonderful energizing food for young children. Packed with antioxidants, known as flavonoids, and beta-carotene, parsley provides protection to cells, helps lower inflammation and supports immune health. It is also thought to be a diuretic, assisting kidney function and reducing fluid retention.

Topped with a delicious herbed cheese, these make a sensational breakfast that will be enjoyed by babies and toddlers alike.

1 small baking potato
1 parsnip, peeled and grated
1 shallot, grated
2 tablespoons butter
2 tablespoons olive oil or melted coconut oil
scant ½ cup regular cottage cheese
1 tablespoon chopped parsley
1 tablespoon capers, rinsed and drained
freshly ground black pepper

1 Coarsely grate the potato onto a clean dish towel and squeeze out the excess moisture. Tip into a bowl and add the parsnip and shallot. Melt the butter in a small pan and stir into the mixture. Season with pepper.

2 Heat the oil in a frying pan. Shape the mixture into 4 patties and put in the pan. Press down with a spatula and cook until golden and crisp, about 5 minutes per side.

3 Mix together the cottage cheese, parsley and capers. Season with a little black pepper.

4 Transfer the rostis to plates and top each one with a little of the herbed cheese. Serve hot.

mexican corn fritters

These lightly spiced fritters are an easy way to introduce children to new flavors and to spices. Delicious hot or cold, they can be served with a little chili or tomato sauce.For a more substantial brunch dish, accompany with some ham or eggs.

SERVES 4

PREPARATION + COOKING
15 + 18 minutes

STORAGE
Keep in the fridge for 1 day.

SERVE THIS WITH...
lean ham or meaty fresh link sausages

3 tablespoons fine cornmeal
½ cup all-purpose flour
pinch of salt
4 teaspoons baking powder
1 tablespoon butter
1 egg, beaten
⅓ cup milk

½ teaspoon dried chili flakes
pinch of smoked paprika
1 tablespoon chopped cilantro
heaped ¾ cup frozen corn
  kernels, thawed
3 tablespoons olive oil or
  melted coconut oil

1 Mix together the cornmeal, flour, salt and baking powder in a bowl.
2 Melt the butter in a small pan, then add to the bowl with the egg and milk and whisk to form a batter. Add the chili flakes, paprika and cilantro, then stir in the corn.
3 Heat the oil in a frying pan and add 4 tablespoonfuls of the mixture to the pan to form 4 little fritters. Cook until browned, 2 to 3 minutes per side. Remove from the pan and keep warm while you make more fritters, 12 in total. Serve hot.

HEALTH BENEFITS
Corn is packed full of brain-boosting and energizing B vitamins, including thiamine (B1), pantothenic acid (B5) and folate. Thiamine is critical for cognitive function, because it is needed for the synthesis of acetylcholine, a neurotransmitter essential for memory. Corn is also a great source of energizing magnesium, manganese and immune-supporting vitamin C.

avocado bagel melts

HEALTH BENEFITS
Nutrient-dense avocados are the perfect food for young children, being rich in monounsaturated fat, which is easily digested, plus energizing B vitamins. A good source of protective antioxidants, including vitamins A, C and E, avocados are a great food for maintaining healthy skin.

These delicious quick bites use wholegrain or seeded bagels to help sustain energy levels through the morning. Topped with mozzarella for protein, plus nutrient-dense avocado, this is a super-healthy fast-food option.

2 tablespoons sun-dried tomato pesto
2 wholewheat or seeded bagels, split in half horizontally
2 tablespoons mayonnaise

1 small ripe avocado, halved, pitted and diced
2 plum (roma) tomatoes, diced
scant ½ cup shredded mozzarella cheese

SERVES 4

PREPARATION + COOKING
10 + 5 minutes

STORAGE
Best eaten immediately.

SERVE THIS WITH...
1 handful of spinach

1 Preheat the broiler.

2 Spread the tomato pesto over the cut sides of the bagels.

3 Mix together the mayonnaise, avocado and tomatoes in a bowl. Spoon the mixture on top of each bagel and sprinkle with the mozzarella.

4 Broil, 4 to 5 inches from the heat, until the cheese melts, about 5 minutes. Serve warm.

SERVES 4

PREPARATION + COOKING
10 + 8 minutes

STORAGE
Keep in the fridge for 1 day.

SERVE THIS WITH...
broiled tomatoes
broiled mushrooms

HEALTH BENEFITS
Eggs really are the perfect breakfast food to start your child's day—a complete source of high-quality protein, plus energizing B vitamins, selenium, iodine, vitamin D and iron. They are also rich in the nutrient choline, used by the body to produce the neurotransmitter acetylcholine, involved in cognitive function and memory.

omelet roll-ups

These little rolls are filled with flakes of hot-smoked salmon and cream cheese, making this an incredibly energizing and brain-boosting dish.

4 eggs
1 tablespoon olive oil or melted coconut oil
½ cup flaked hot-smoked salmon

1 tablespoon chopped dill
¼ cup cream cheese
freshly ground black pepper

1 Beat the eggs in a bowl and season with black pepper.
2 Heat half the oil in a small omelet pan and pour in half of the beaten eggs. Swirl the eggs around the pan and cook until the base of the omelet is lightly set. Push the set parts of the omelet into the uncooked center and continue cooking until the omelet is set and lightly golden on the underside.
3 Flip the omelet over and brown the other side lightly for a few seconds. Turn out onto a cutting board. Repeat with the remaining eggs to make a second omelet.
4 Mix together the salmon, dill and cream cheese in a bowl. Season with a little pepper. Spread the mixture on one side of each omelet, leaving the edges clear.
5 Roll up each omelet tightly and cut across into slices. Serve warm or cold.

cheesy-chili muffins

Here's a spicy savory option for breakfast. You can vary the amount of chili sauce you use to suit your child's taste.

light olive oil, for greasing
1¼ cups self-rising white flour
1 cup self-rising wholewheat flour
2 tablespoons sweet chili sauce
2 eggs, beaten
1 cup plus 1 tablespoon buttermilk

2½ ounces butter
5 ounces Cheddar cheese: about one-third grated and the rest cut into 10 little cubes
1 cup frozen corn, thawed
1 plum (roma) tomato, diced

MAKES 10

PREPARATION + COOKING
15 + 20 minutes

STORAGE
Keep in the fridge for 2 days or freeze for up to 1 month.

SERVE THIS WITH...
baked beans
broiled mushrooms

HEALTH BENEFITS
Chilies not only give a wonderful spicy heat to foods, but are also rich in antioxidant vitamins A (beta-carotene), C and E as well as folic acid and potassium. Great for stimulating circulation, they also have mild analgesic properties that may be useful in helping to ease headaches and also sinusitis.

1 Preheat the oven to 400°F. Lightly grease 10 cups in a muffin pan.

2 Mix the flours together in a bowl.

3 Beat together the sweet chili sauce, eggs and buttermilk. Melt the butter in a small pan and add to the mixture, then stir into the flour. Mix in half the grated cheese, the corn and tomato.

4 Spoon 1 tablespoon of the batter into each muffin cup. Put a cube of cheese in the center, cover with more batter and sprinkle the remaining grated cheese on top.

5 Bake until the muffins are golden and have risen, about 20 minutes. Unmold onto a wire rack and let cool slightly. Serve warm.

LUNCHES

Keep your child focused and alert all afternoon with a nutritious, satisfying lunch. Whether you are looking for packed lunch ideas beyond the humble sandwich, or finger foods straight from the oven, in this chapter you will find a whole range of delicious and nourishing dishes to enjoy. Designed with busy parents in mind, they can be prepared in advance and, being finger foods, are perfect for days out. Many of the recipes are ideal for picnics, brunches and parties, too. Whether you are rushing around or have a little more time to spare, by providing your children with a nourishing lunch, you can boost their energy levels, helping them to make the most of their day.

peanut chicken bites

These are moist, crisp and incredibly healthy.

SERVES 4

PREPARATION + COOKING
20 + 30 minutes + chilling

STORAGE
Keep in the fridge for 2 days.

SERVE THIS WITH…
Raita (see page 58)
steamed vegetables
sweet potato wedges, baked in
  olive oil
Peaches with Berry Syrup
  (see page 128)

HEALTH BENEFITS
Garlic is a wonderful protective
food for children: being a
natural antibiotic, it can help to
protect from bacterial and fungal
infections. A useful decongestant
and immune-supporting spice,
it is a great choice for relieving
symptoms of coughs and colds.
Rich in sulfurous compounds,
it helps to stimulate liver
detoxification. In addition, it is
beneficial for skin conditions
such as eczema.

3 tablespoons Greek yogurt	4 skinless, boneless chicken
1 tablespoon lemon juice	thighs, cut in half
1 garlic clove, minced	scant 1¼ cups roasted unsalted
½ teaspoon ground cumin	peanuts
½ teaspoon garam masala	¼ cup dried shredded coconut
or mango powder	light olive oil, for greasing

1 Put the yogurt, lemon juice, garlic, cumin and garam masala in a bowl and whisk to combine. Add the chicken thighs and toss to coat in the mixture, then cover and let marinate in the fridge for 30 minutes.

2 Put the peanuts in a food processor and process into coarse crumbs. Tip onto a plate and mix with the coconut.

3 Preheat the oven to 400°F. Lightly grease a baking sheet and line it with parchment paper.

4 Coat the chicken thighs completely in the peanut mixture and put on the prepared baking sheet. Bake until golden brown and cooked through, 20 to 30 minutes.

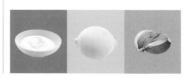

chicken turnovers

These little pastries are healthy and portable.

1 tablespoon olive oil,
    plus extra for greasing
½ red onion, minced
1 garlic clove, minced
6 ounces lean ground chicken
3½ ounces broccoli, diced
1 tablespoon tomato paste
¾ cup canned corn kernels,
    drained

freshly ground black pepper
1 egg, beaten

PASTRY
scant 1½ cups all-purpose
    flour, plus extra for dusting
1 tablespoon ground flaxseed
5 tablespoons chilled unsalted
    butter, diced

SERVES 4

PREPARATION + COOKING
20 + 25 minutes + chilling

STORAGE
Keep in the fridge for 2 days.

SERVE THIS WITH...
coleslaw
mixed salad
Mango Ice Pops (see page 124)

HEALTH BENEFITS
Cruciferous vegetables, such
as broccoli, are superfoods for
your children. They are packed
with powerful phytonutrient
antioxidants, such as
sulphoraphane and indoles, as
well as beta-carotene, which can
help protect against cell damage,
support liver function and
promote a healthy respiratory
tract and skin. Broccoli is also
a good source of folic acid and
iron, which are important for
hemoglobin production and
healthy red blood cells.

1 To make the pastry, sift the flour and flaxseed into a
large bowl. Rub in the butter until you have a soft crumb
texture. Add enough cold water to form a firm dough.
Shape into a ball, wrap and chill for 30 minutes.
2 Heat the oil in a frying pan and sauté the onion and garlic.
Add the chicken and brown. Add the broccoli, tomato
paste, corn and pepper. Stir for 2 minutes, then cool.
3 Preheat the oven to 400°F. Roll out the pastry and cut
out 8 rounds with a 4-inch cutter. Put a spoonful of filling
in the center of each round. Brush the edge with water,
then fold the pastry over the filling and pinch to seal.
4 Put the turnovers on an oiled baking sheet and brush
with beaten egg. Bake until browned, 20 to 25 minutes.

tandoori chicken strips

Lightly spiced strips of tender chicken breast.

PREPARATION + COOKING
20 + 20 minutes + chilling

STORAGE
Keep in the fridge for 1 day.

SERVE THIS WITH...
strips of naan bread
Raita (see page 58)
wilted spinach
homemade dahl
Coconut Squares (see page 127)

HEALTH BENEFITS
Yogurt is a good protein food,
rich in amino acids such as
tyrosine to boost alertness,
mood and concentration. It is
also a useful source of calcium
plus "friendly" bacteria known to
help promote healthy digestion,
immune health and absorption
of nutrients.

9 ounces skinless, boneless
   chicken breast halves
1 teaspoon chaat masala spice
   powder
1 teaspoon lemon juice

MARINADE
1 cup plain yogurt

1 teaspoon garam masala
½ teaspoon mild chili powder
pinch of salt
2 tablespoons lemon juice
1 garlic clove
¾-inch piece fresh gingerroot,
   peeled

1 Put all the ingredients for the marinade in a mini-chopper or blender and blend until smooth.

2 Score the chicken breasts lightly with a sharp knife and put them in a container with a tight-fitting lid. Pour the marinade over the chicken and rub in well. Let marinate in the fridge for at least 20 minutes or overnight.

3 Preheat the oven to 400°F. Put the chicken on a nonstick baking sheet and bake for 5 minutes. Reduce the heat to 350°F and bake until the chicken is golden and cooked through (the juices should run clear when the thickest part is pierced with a skewer), 10 to 15 minutes.

4 Remove from the oven and let rest for 5 minutes. Sprinkle with the chaat masala and lemon juice, then slice the chicken into strips.

chicken yakitori sticks

A sensational Asian-style chicken dish.

9 ounces skinless, boneless
    chicken breast, cut into
    thin strips
4 tablespoons mirin
2 tablespoons kecap manis
2 teaspoons low-salt soy sauce
finely grated zest of 1 lemon
    and 1 tablespoon juice
3 tablespoons rice wine
    vinegar
2 tablespoons raw cane sugar
    or xylitol
1 teaspoon toasted sesame
    seeds

SERVES 4

PREPARATION + COOKING
15 + 13 minutes + chilling

STORAGE
Keep in the fridge for 1 day.

SERVE THIS WITH...
stir-fried vegetables
rice noodles
Frozen Pineapple Cheesecake
  Slice (see page 138)

HEALTH BENEFITS
Sesame seeds are a good source
of calcium and magnesium,
plus B vitamins, which can
help to calm your child and
aid relaxation of nerve and
muscle cells. They are also
rich in immune-supporting
zinc, antioxidant vitamin E and
omega-6 fatty acids, which are
beneficial for healthy skin.

1 Put the chicken in a shallow dish. Combine the mirin, kecap manis and soy sauce and pour over the chicken. Let marinate in the fridge for 2 to 3 hours or overnight.

2 About 30 minutes before cooking, soak 8 mini wooden skewers in water. Thread the chicken strips onto the skewers, reserving the marinade.

3 Preheat the broiler. Broil the chicken, 4 to 5 inches from the heat, turning frequently, until cooked through (the juices should run clear when it is pierced in the thickest part with a skewer), 7 to 8 minutes.

4 Meanwhile, pour the reserved marinade into a small pan. Add the lemon zest and juice, vinegar and sugar and bring to a boil. Simmer until syrupy, about 5 minutes. Stir in the sesame seeds and pour into a small bowl. Let cool.

5 Remove the skewers. Serve with the dipping sauce.

duck lettuce wraps

Healthy and delicious protein-rich wraps.

PREPARATION + COOKING
20 + 20 minutes

STORAGE
Keep the duck in the fridge for
1 day and the chutney for 4 days.

SERVE THIS WITH...
cucumber and bell pepper sticks
Chunky Breadsticks (see
page 87)
Summer Berry Ice Cups
(see page 125)

HEALTH BENEFITS
Duck breast is an excellent
source of lean protein, containing
all the essential amino acids
needed by growing children. It is
also packed with iron, zinc and
B vitamins, required for energy
production and keeping your
child alert and focused. And it is
a good source of selenium: an
important mineral for a healthy
immune system and thyroid
function.

2 duck breasts
1 tablespoon low-salt soy sauce
2 teaspoons honey or
   agave nectar
4 large romaine leaves
1 tablespoon toasted sesame
   seeds

CHUTNEY
⅓ cup raw cane sugar or xylitol
1 star anise
½ teaspoon ground cinnamon
¾ cup dried cranberries
2 cups frozen cranberries
juice of 1 orange

1 Preheat the oven to 400°F.
2 Remove any fat from the duck. Mix together the
soy sauce and honey and rub over the duck. Heat a
frying pan and sear the duck for 2 minutes on each side.
Transfer to a roasting pan and roast until cooked through,
12 to 15 minutes. Let cool, then slice into strips.
3 To make the chutney, put the sugar, spices and
4 tablespoons water in a pan and bring to a boil. Add
the cranberries and juice and simmer for 5 to 6 minutes,
mashing down the fruit to form a soft purée. Let cool.
4 To assemble, put a few slices of duck in the center of a
lettuce leaf. Spoon a little chutney on top and add some
sesame seeds. Fold the lettuce leaf over the filling and roll
up, folding in the sides as you roll to form a wrap.

pork & apple burgers

Lean ground pork with grated apple create simple moist burgers that are packed with flavor. Babies and older children love them.

light olive oil, for drizzling and greasing
9 ounces lean ground pork
1 shallot, minced
1 garlic clove, minced

1 tablespoon chopped cilantro
1 apple, peeled, cored and grated
2 teaspoons cornstarch

1 Preheat the oven to 400°F. Lightly grease a baking sheet and line it with parchment paper.
2 Put all the ingredients in a large bowl and mix well. With lightly oiled hands, shape the mixture into 8 small burgers. Put them on the prepared baking sheet and drizzle a little olive oil over them.
3 Bake, turning them over halfway through cooking so that they are golden brown all over, 20 to 25 minutes.
4 To serve, put a burger in a lettuce leaf and top with a little tomato sauce.

SERVES 4

PREPARATION + COOKING
20 + 25 minutes

STORAGE
Keep in the fridge for 2 days.

SERVE THIS WITH...
romaine heart leaves
sliced tomatoes
Tomato Chutney (see page 105)
coleslaw
mixed salad
fresh fruit salad

HEALTH BENEFITS
Coriander is a versatile herb, in that both the leaves (called cilantro) and seeds can be used in dishes. Known for its antibacterial properties, it is effective in protecting against bacterial infections, promoting digestion and relieving intestinal gas and stomach upsets. Being rich in antioxidants, it also has beneficial anti-inflammatory properties.

baked ham & egg cups

Eggs baked in a basket of lean ham and topped with tomato creates a fun hand-sized quiche— but without the pastry.

SERVES 4

PREPARATION + COOKING
10 + 8 minutes

STORAGE
Keep in the fridge for 1 day.

SERVE THIS WITH...
mixed salad
Squash Scones (see page 82)
fresh fruit

HEALTH BENEFITS
When choosing cooked ham, look for 100% meat, without colors, additives or fillers. For small children, it is important to watch the sodium content, so aim for meats with less than 0.25g sodium per 100g. There are also some excellent nitrate-free meats available.

light olive oil, for greasing
4 slices of lean ham
2 tomatoes, finely diced
Tabasco sauce (optional)

4 eggs
½ cup grated Cheddar cheese
freshly ground black pepper

1 Preheat the oven to 400°F.
2 Lightly grease 4 cups in a muffin pan. Put a slice of ham in each cup so that it lines it completely and rises above the top edge.
3 Divide the tomatoes among the cups and season with a dash of Tabasco, if using. Carefully break an egg into the center of each cup. Season with black pepper, then sprinkle the grated cheese on top.
4 Bake until the eggs are just set and the cheese has melted, 5 to 8 minutes. Let cool slightly before serving.

pigs in blankets

Crisp and golden little pigs in blankets are perfect for children on the go.

1 tablespoon light olive oil, plus extra for greasing
4 meaty fresh pork link sausages
1 shallot, chopped
½ cup all-purpose flour

scant ⅔ cup lowfat (2%) milk
1 egg, beaten
2 teaspoons Dijon mustard
1 teaspoon chopped thyme
freshly ground black pepper

1 Preheat the oven to 400°F.

2 Lightly grease 4 cups in a large muffin pan.

3 Heat the oil in a frying pan and fry the sausages until golden brown and cooked through, about 5 minutes. About 1 minute before the end of the cooking time, add the shallot and sauté until soft. Let the sausages cool a little, then cut into chunks. Put in a bowl with the shallot.

4 Combine the flour, milk, egg and mustard in a blender and blend to form a smooth batter. Season with a little pepper and stir in the thyme.

5 Put the muffin pan in the oven to heat up for 2 to 3 minutes. Remove from the oven and divide the sausage mixture among the cups. Pour in the batter. Return to the oven and bake until risen and golden brown, about 20 minutes. Let cool slightly before serving.

SERVES 4

PREPARATION + COOKING
15 + 25 minutes

STORAGE
Keep in the fridge for 1 day.

SERVE THIS WITH...
baked beans
steamed vegetables
Lemon Cheesecake
  (see page 133)
fresh berries

HEALTH BENEFITS
Sausages can be a relatively healthy option if you choose those with a high meat content. As they are already seasoned, avoid using additional salt— instead flavor with herbs and spices and mustard.

lamb-stuffed peppers

SERVES 4

PREPARATION + COOKING
20 + 30 minutes

STORAGE
Keep in the fridge for 2 days.

SERVE THIS WITH…
sweet potato wedges baked in a little olive oil
mixed salad
fresh fruit
plain yogurt

HEALTH BENEFITS
The healthy monounsaturated fats in olives, together with their phenol content, make them wonderfully protective foods useful for reducing inflammation, which can be helpful for conditions such as asthma and eczema. Packed with healthy fats, they help to slow down the rate of release of glucose into the bloodstream, helping to balance energy levels through the day.

This Spanish-inspired dish uses pepper halves as shells for the tangy lamb and olive filling.

1 tablespoon olive or melted coconut oil, plus extra for greasing
1 shallot, minced
2 garlic cloves, minced
¾ cup ground lamb
½ teaspoon ground cumin
pinch of dried chili flakes
pinch of ground cloves
8 pitted black olives, chopped
1 tablespoon pine nuts
¼ cup tomato purée
2 red bell peppers, halved and seeded
freshly ground black pepper

1 Preheat the oven to 400°F. Grease a baking sheet.

2 Heat the oil in a large frying pan and sauté the shallot and garlic until soft, about 2 minutes. Add the lamb and spices and stir until the lamb is cooked through, about 10 minutes. Mix in the olives, pine nuts and purée.

3 Put the bell pepper halves in a pan of boiling water and blanch for 2 to 3 minutes to soften slightly. Drain and dry on paper towels.

4 Put the pepper halves on the prepared baking sheet. Fill with the lamb mixture and season with black pepper.

5 Bake until the peppers are lightly golden around the edges, about 15 minutes. Let cool slightly before serving.

baked phyllo rolls

These are much healthier than the fried version.

1 teaspoon cornstarch
2 teaspoons rice wine vinegar
2 teaspoons low-salt soy sauce
1 egg white, beaten
7 ounces lean boneless lamb,
   sliced into thin strips
1 tablespoon light olive oil,
   plus extra for greasing and
   brushing

¾-inch piece fresh gingerroot,
   peeled and grated
1 garlic clove, minced
9 ounces mixed stir-fry
   vegetables, thawed if frozen
2 tablespoons sweet chili sauce
8 phyllo pastry sheets, cut in
   half to make 16 squares

1 Preheat the oven to 425°F. Grease a baking sheet.
2 Mix the cornstarch, vinegar, soy sauce and egg white with enough water to form a paste. Toss the lamb in this.
3 Heat the oil in a frying pan and sauté the ginger, garlic and lamb until the meat starts to brown, 3 to 4 minutes. Add the vegetables and sweet chili sauce, plus a little water if too dry. Fry until the lamb is cooked. Let cool.
4 Lay a square of phyllo with one point facing you. Brush with oil, then put another square on top. Put 1 teaspoon of the filling in the center of the pastry. Roll up, folding in the sides as you roll. Repeat to make 8 rolls.
5 Put seam-side down on the baking sheet. Brush with oil. Bake until golden and crisp, 15 to 20 minutes. Serve.

SERVES 8

PREPARATION + COOKING
20 + 30 minutes

STORAGE
Keep in the fridge for 2 days.

SERVE THIS WITH...
cucumber and bell pepper sticks
Tomato Chutney (see page 105)
Grilled Pineapple (see page 130)
plain yogurt

HEALTH BENEFITS
Ginger is a well-known digestive aid and a useful remedy for nausea as well as indigestion and stomach upsets. If your child suffers with sinus problems or frequent coughs and colds, including ginger in their diet can stimulate circulation and help expel phlegm. Rich in powerful plant phytonutrients known as gingerols, it also has anti-inflammatory action and may help to alleviate conditions such as asthma and sinusitis.

SERVES 4

PREPARATION + COOKING
15 + 10 minutes

STORAGE
Keep in the fridge for 1 day.

SERVE THIS WITH...
shredded lettuce
sliced tomatoes
coleslaw
Frozen Blueberry & Chocolate
  Slice (see page 135)

HEALTH BENEFITS
Lean beef is a good source of
protein, energizing B vitamins
and iron. B vitamins are also
essential for the production of
neurotransmitters, which are
essential for brain function and
memory. Beef also provides
plenty of zinc, which is often
low in children's diets and an
important mineral for wound-
healing and immune support.

steak gremolata rolls

This simple dish, packed with protein and
energizing lean beef, is great for when your
child's energy levels are low.

finely grated zest of 1 lemon
1 garlic clove, minced
1 small handful of flat-leaf
  parsley, minced
2 tablespoons light olive oil

2 minute steaks, about
  4 ounces each
8 cherry tomatoes, quartered
4 wholewheat bread rolls

1 Put the lemon, garlic, parsley and 1 tablespoon of the
oil in a bowl and mix well.
2 Heat the remaining oil in a large frying pan. Put the
steaks in the pan and cook until browned and cooked
through, 3 to 4 minutes per side. Just before the end of
the cooking time, add the tomatoes to the pan and cook
briefly to soften.
3 Remove the steaks from the pan and sprinkle half of
the parsley mixture over them. Let the steaks rest for
5 minutes, then slice them thinly.
4 Cut the rolls in half and toast the cut sides lightly.
5 Put a little shredded lettuce on the bottom half of each
roll and pile the steak slices and tomatoes on the lettuce.
Sprinkle the remaining parsley mixture over and put the
toasted tops of the rolls in place.

tostada chili wedges

Corn tortillas filled with beef and refried beans.

1 tablespoon olive oil, plus
    extra for brushing
1 small red onion, minced
1 red chili (mildly hot or hot, to
    taste), seeded and minced
2 garlic cloves, minced
6 ounces lean ground beef
14 ounces canned kidney
    beans, drained and rinsed

1 tomato, chopped
½ teaspoon low-sodium
    vegetable bouillon powder,
    dissolved in 4 tablespoons
    hot water
4 corn tortillas
½ cup grated Cheddar cheese

SERVES 4

PREPARATION + COOKING
15 + 25 minutes

STORAGE
Keep in the fridge for 1 day.

SERVE THIS WITH...
mixed salad
Raita (see page 58)
Mango Ice Pops
    (see page 124)

HEALTH BENEFITS
Kidney beans are a great
vegetarian source of protein.
They are rich in folate and iron,
both of which are important for
maintaining energy levels and
the production of the immune
system's antibodies and white
blood cells. Beans also contain
high levels of fiber, which helps
ensure a healthy digestion and
alleviate constipation.

1 Heat the oil in a frying pan and sauté the onion, chili
and garlic for 2 minutes. Add the beef and continue to
cook until it is browned, 6 to 8 minutes.
2 Add the beans and cook until hot, 2 to 3 minutes.
Use a potato masher to break up the beans.
3 Add the tomato and vegetable bouillon to the beef
mixture. Continue to cook for about 5 minutes.
4 Preheat the broiler. Put 2 tortillas on a baking sheet
and spoon the beef mixture over them. Sprinkle with the
cheese. Put the other tortillas on top and press down
lightly. Brush the top with oil.
5 Toast the tortilla sandwiches under the broiler until
golden and the cheese has melted, about 5 minutes.
Cut into wedges and serve hot.

029

fruity salmon skewers

HEALTH BENEFITS

Wild salmon is one of the healthiest foods for your child's brain, being a great source of the omega-3 fats known as DHA and EPA, which are essential for cognitive function and memory and may also boost mood. Salmon is also a great source of protein, helping to support growth and development and to stabilize blood sugar levels through the day—important if you want your child to stay focused and energized. The omega-3 oils are also anti-inflammatory, so can be useful for skin conditions such as eczema.

Mini squares of broiled salmon with cubes of fresh pineapple create a sensational little dish accompanied by a sweet and tangy chutney. Keeping the fish bite-sized is a great way to encourage even babies to try something new, too. This dish can be served hot or cold.

8 ounces skinless salmon fillet,
cut into 8 cubes
¼ pineapple, peeled, cored
and cut into 8 cubes
1 tablespoon honey

CHUTNEY
1 tablespoon olive oil
¾-inch piece fresh gingerroot,
peeled and grated

1 garlic clove, minced
1 shallot, minced
4 tablespoons cider vinegar
14 ounces canned crushed
tomatoes
pinch of ground cinnamon
pinch of ground cloves
2 tablespoons raw cane sugar
or xylitol

SERVES 4

PREPARATION + COOKING
30 + 40 minutes + marinating

STORAGE
Keep the fish in the fridge for
1 day and the chutney for 4 days.

SERVE THIS WITH...
coleslaw
mixed salad

1 To make the chutney, heat the oil and sauté the ginger and garlic for 1 minute. Add the other ingredients and bring to a boil. Simmer, stirring occasionally, until thick, about 30 minutes. Let cool.

2 Put the salmon in a shallow dish and spoon a little of the chutney over. Let marinate in the fridge for 30 minutes.

3 Soak 8 mini wooden skewers in water. Heat the broiler.

4 Thread the pineapple and salmon onto each skewer and spread on a nonstick baking sheet. Drizzle honey over the pineapple. Broil until the salmon is golden and cooked, 5 to 6 minutes. Remove the skewers before serving, with the rest of the chutney.

creamy trout pitas

This creamy fish pâté is perfect as a sandwich filler, spread on little strips of toast or used to stuff mini pitas or baby potatoes. Smoked trout has a mild flavor, making it a popular choice for children and an ideal option if you're looking to increase their intake of oily fish.

7 ounces hot-smoked trout
   fillets, skinned
¼ cup crème fraîche
finely grated zest and juice of
   ½ lemon

1 small handful of dill, chopped
4 mini wholewheat pita breads
1 tomato, finely diced
freshly ground black pepper

1 Put the trout, crème fraîche, lemon zest and juice and dill in a food processor and pulse to form a chunky paste. Do not over-process. Season with a little black pepper.
2 Warm the pitas briefly in a toaster so they puff up slightly. Split the pittas along one side and spread a generous amount of the trout pâté inside each one. Scatter a little diced tomato over and close to serve.

easy sushi rolls

These rolls contain avocado and vegetables.

1 large, ripe avocado, pitted
1 teaspoon low-salt soy sauce
2 teaspoons lemon juice
pinch of ground cumin
4 nori sheets
¼ hothouse cucumber, seeded and cut into strips
½ red bell pepper, thinly sliced
1 handful of alfalfa sprouts

DIPPING SAUCE
½ cup cashew nut butter or other nut butter
2 tablespoons lemon juice
1 tablespoon raw cane sugar or xylitol
2 tablespoons low-salt soy sauce
1 garlic clove, crushed

1 Spoon the avocado flesh into a bowl. Add the soy sauce, lemon juice and cumin and stir together until smooth.

2 Put a nori sheet shiny-side down on a sushi mat. Spread the avocado thinly over the sheet, leaving a ¾-inch strip clear at one end.

3 Put a line of cucumber, bell pepper and alfalfa across the upper half of the sheet. Using your fingers, dampen the edge of the sheet with water. Using the mat, roll up the sheet and put the roll seam-side down on a board. Repeat with the other sheets and remaining fillings. Using a sharp, serrated knife, slice each roll across into 6.

4 Put the dipping sauce ingredients in a blender and blend until smooth, adding up to 4 tablespoons of water to form a thick dipping consistency. Serve the rolls with the sauce.

SERVES 4

PREPARATION
20 minutes

STORAGE
Best eaten immediately. Keep the sauce in the fridge for 3 days.

SERVE THIS WITH...
strips of cucumber and bell pepper
tamari soy sauce, for dipping
Grilled Pineapple (see page 130)
plain yogurt

HEALTH BENEFITS
Sea vegetables are one of the richest sources of essential minerals, making them an excellent nutrient-dense food. Packed with iodine, which is important for the normal functioning of the thyroid gland and metabolism, they are also rich in folic acid, which is needed for the formation of healthy red blood cells, and magnesium, which acts as a natural relaxant and calming mineral.

crisp spiced shrimp

These juicy shrimp have a tasty crisp crust.

SERVES 4

PREPARATION + COOKING
15 + 7 minutes + marinating

STORAGE
Keep in the fridge for 1 day.

SERVE THIS WITH...
strips of naan bread
steamed vegetables
Coconut Squares (see page 127)

HEALTH BENEFITS
Shrimp are a surprisingly good source of omega-3 fatty acids, which are important for a child's brain development and also valuable to maintain a healthy immune system and healthy skin. They contain high levels of immune-supporting minerals, especially zinc and selenium, plus plenty of high-quality protein—essential for the production of white blood cells.

2 tablespoons tikka paste
2 tablespoons Greek yogurt
2 teaspoons lime juice
16 raw extra-large shrimp, peeled
light olive oil, for greasing
½ cup fine cornmeal

RAITA
scant 1 cup Greek yogurt
1 handful of mint leaves
1 handful of cilantro
¼ hothouse cucumber, peeled and seeded
freshly ground black pepper

1 Put the tikka paste, yogurt and lime juice in a container and mix well. Add the shrimp and turn to coat. Cover and let marinate in the fridge for 30 minutes. Meanwhile, soak 8 wooden skewers in water.
2 To make the raita, blend the yogurt with the herbs in a food processor. Grate the cucumber and squeeze the flesh to remove as much liquid as possible, then add it to the yogurt mixture. Season with black pepper. Cover and chill.
3 Preheat the broiler. Lightly grease a baking sheet.
4 Put the cornmeal on a plate. Remove the shrimp from the marinade and coat in the cornmeal, shaking off the excess. Thread 2 shrimp onto each skewer and lay on the baking sheet. Broil, turning occasionally, until golden, crisp and cooked, 6 to 7 minutes. Remove the skewers and serve the prawns with the raita.

ricotta, pear & walnut sandwiches

This is a wonderful sweet, nutritious sandwich option, combining protein-rich cheese, ripe pears and brain-boosting walnuts. The filling is great for wraps and pita breads, too, and also makes a wonderful topping for wholewheat bagels for an afternoon snack.

2 ripe pears, cored and diced
pinch of ground cinnamon
scant 1 cup ricotta cheese

2 tablespoons chopped walnuts
8 slices of wholewheat bread

1 Put the pears, cinnamon, cheese and walnuts in a bowl and toss gently to mix.
2 Spread the mixture over half the slices of bread and top with the remaining slices. Cut the sandwiches into halves or quarters to serve.

SERVES 4

PREPARATION
10 minutes

STORAGE
Keep in the fridge for 1 day.

SERVE THIS WITH...
vegetable sticks
fresh fruit
Zucchini & Apple Cake
(see page 84)

HEALTH BENEFITS
Walnuts are the best nuts because of their high omega-3 content, and they have long been regarded as a "brain food." Omega-3 essential fats are vital for the health and function of brain cells and have been shown to improve mood, learning and behavior in children. Try to eat them raw to retain as much of the essential fats as possible.

034

tofu & cashew burgers

These protein-packed vegetarian burgers are perfect as an energizing lunch.

MAKES 12

PREPARATION + COOKING
15 + 25 minutes

STORAGE
Keep in the fridge for 3 days.

SERVE THIS WITH...
mixed salad leaves
wholewheat bread rolls
Tomato Chutney (see page 105)
fresh fruit
Almond Linzer Cookies
   (see page 75)

HEALTH BENEFITS
Button mushrooms are a good source of antioxidants, copper, zinc and selenium, which are all important for a healthy immune system. They also contain important polysaccharides and beta-glucans—well known for supporting immune function and the production of white blood cells and antibodies. They are also a useful brain food, rich in B vitamins.

2 garlic cloves, peeled
1 small red onion, chopped
3 tablespoons olive oil or
   melted coconut oil
3½ ounces button mushrooms,
   minced
1 small carrot, peeled and
   finely grated
1 teaspoon smoked paprika
½ cup roasted, unsalted
   cashew nuts
9 ounces firm tofu, drained

1 Put the garlic and onion in a food processor and blitz until minced. Heat 1 tablespoon of the oil in a frying pan and sauté the garlic and onion until soft but not brown, 2 to 3 minutes.

2 Add the mushrooms, carrot and paprika to the pan and cook until soft, 2 to 3 minutes. Pour the vegetables into a strainer to drain off any excess moisture.

3 Put the nuts in a grinder or food processor and blitz until finely ground. Put the tofu in the food processor and pulse briefly until crumbly.

4 Combine the vegetables, nuts and tofu in a bowl and season with pepper. Shape into 12 little patties.

5 Heat the remaining oil in a frying pan and fry the patties, in 2 batches, until they are golden brown, 3 to 4 minutes per side.

babaganoush with pita triangles

A tasty twist on the classic Middle-Eastern dip.

1 tablespoon light olive oil,
   plus extra for greasing
2 eggplants
2 garlic cloves, peeled
juice of ½ lemon
scant ⅔ cup crumbled goat
   cheese
3 heaped tablespoons tahini

1 tablespoon chopped parsley
freshly ground black pepper

PITA TRIANGLES
2 wholewheat pita breads
2 tablespoons light olive oil
pinch of paprika

SERVES 6

PREPARATION + COOKING
20 + 50 minutes

STORAGE
Keep the dip in the fridge for
2 to 3 days. Store the pita
triangles in an airtight container
for 1 day.

SERVE THIS WITH...
vegetable sticks
Choc-Nut Lemon Bars
   (see page 81)
fresh fruit

HEALTH BENEFITS
Eggplant is packed with
antioxidants, phenolic
compounds, such as caffeic and
chlorogenic acid, and flavonoids,
such as nasunin. Nasunin has
been shown to protect the fats in
brain cells from damage, while
chlorogenic acid has a range of
health benefits, including being
antimicrobial and antiviral. A
good source of fiber for healthy
bowel movements, too.

1 Preheat the oven to 375°F. Grease a baking sheet.
2 Prick the eggplants all over and put on the prepared baking sheet. Roast until black and soft, 30 to 40 minutes.
3 Peel off the skin and scoop the flesh into a food processor. Blitz with the remaining ingredients until smooth. Season with black pepper.
4 To make the pita triangles, preheat the broiler. Slice the pitas in half horizontally, then cut into small triangles. Spread them on a baking sheet. Drizzle the oil over and season with paprika and pepper.
5 Broil until crisp, 5 to 8 minutes. Remove from the heat and let cool. Spread the dip on the pita triangles to serve.

quesadilla wedges

HEALTH BENEFITS
Spinach is the perfect energizing food for children, packed with iron, folate, B vitamins, vitamin K and magnesium, which are all important for building healthy blood cells. It is also a great source of the antioxidant vitamins C, E and beta-carotene, which are vital for supporting your child's immune health, plus calcium for building bones.

A fun alternative to a toasted sandwich, these tasty wedges are packed with protein as well as containing plenty of greens, which are a great vegetarian source of iron and B vitamins.

2 tablespoons olive oil or
  melted coconut oil
5½ ounces firm tofu, crumbled
pinch of turmeric
pinch of paprika
1 garlic clove, minced
few drops of Tabasco
2 jarred, roasted red bell
  peppers in oil, drained
  and chopped

2 large handfuls of baby
  spinach leaves
1 tablespoon chopped cilantro
heaped ⅓ cup shredded
  Monterey Jack or mozzarella
  cheese
4 flour tortillas
freshly ground black pepper

SERVES 4

PREPARATION + COOKING
15 + 25 minutes

STORAGE
Keep in the fridge for 1 day.

SERVE THIS WITH...
mixed salad

1 Heat 1 tablespoon of the oil in a frying pan and fry the tofu with the turmeric and paprika for 4 to 5 minutes. Add the garlic and Tabasco and cook for 1 to 2 minutes longer.

2 Stir in the peppers, spinach and remaining oil and sauté until the spinach has wilted, about 1 minute. Season with black pepper and stir in the cilantro.

3 Heat one of the tortillas in a frying pan over low heat for 2 minutes. Spread half the tofu mixture over and then add half the cheese. Firmly press a second tortilla on top.

4 Fry until golden brown and crisp, 2 to 3 minutes per side. Remove from the pan and repeat with the remaining tortillas. Let cool slightly before cutting into wedges.

037

cheese & sun-dried tomato polenta toasts

Crisp little polenta toasts flavored with cheese and tomato make these perfect nutritious bites for small children.

SERVES 4

PREPARATION + COOKING
20 + 30 minutes + chilling

STORAGE
Keep in the fridge for 1 day.

SERVE THIS WITH...
coleslaw or mixed salad
baked beans
Summer Berry Ice Cups
(see page 125)

HEALTH BENEFITS
Polenta is a delicious gluten-free alternative to toast and a rich source of B vitamins, fiber and slow-releasing carbohydrate to help keep your child's energy levels sustained through the day.

1 tablespoon light olive oil,
   plus extra for greasing
3 cups low-sodium vegetable
   stock
scant 1 cup instant polenta
8 sun-dried tomatoes in oil,
   drained and chopped

¼ cup grated Parmesan
   cheese, plus extra for
   sprinkling
olive oil or melted coconut oil,
   for frying

1 Grease an 8-inch square shallow cake pan.
2 Put the stock in a pan and bring to a boil. Gradually add the polenta, stirring constantly. Reduce the heat and simmer, stirring, until thickened, about 10 minutes. Add the 1 tablespoon oil, tomatoes and cheese and beat well.
3 Spread the mixture in the prepared pan and let cool. Cover with plastic wrap and refrigerate until firm, about 2 hours. Unmold the polenta and cut into ¾-inch pieces.
4 Heat some olive oil in a frying pan and fry the polenta pieces, in batches, until brown, 2 to 3 minutes per side. Sprinkle with a little extra Parmesan before serving.

mediterranean potato cakes

Rich and full of flavor, these little potato cakes are delicious hot or cold.

9 ounces boiling potatoes, peeled and cut into chunks
½ cup sliced pitted black olives
1 jarred, roasted red bell pepper in oil, drained and minced
heaped ⅓ cup grated Parmesan cheese
1 tablespoon minced basil
½ cup all-purpose flour
2 eggs, beaten
2 cups fine wholewheat bread crumbs
light olive oil, for greasing
freshly ground black pepper

1 Put the potatoes in a large pan of boiling water. Simmer until tender, 12 to 15 minutes, then drain well. Pass through a potato ricer or mash. It should be quite dry.
2 Add the olives, bell pepper, Parmesan and basil to the potato and mix well. Season with black pepper.
3 Put the flour, eggs and bread crumbs on three separate plates. Shape the potato mixture into little patties. Roll in the flour, then dip into the egg and, finally, coat with the bread crumbs. Chill for 30 minutes.
4 Preheat the oven to 425°F. Lightly grease a baking sheet. Put the potato cakes on the sheet and bake until golden and crisp, about 20 minutes.

SERVES 4

PREPARATION + COOKING
15 + 35 minutes + chilling

STORAGE
Keep in the fridge for 2 days. Freeze uncooked cakes for up to 1 month, then cook from frozen.

SERVE THIS WITH...
steamed vegetables
fresh meat or vegetarian sausages
Peaches with Berry Syrup (see page 128)

HEALTH BENEFITS
Parmesan cheese is an excellent source of protein and rich in bone-building phosphorous and calcium. It also provides plenty of vitamins B12 and B2, zinc and selenium. It is full of flavor but high in salt, so use in small amounts to enhance the taste and nutritional profile of a dish.

039

bean & cheese bites

Using canned lima beans makes these little bites a very easy recipe. The Middle-Eastern spice sumac adds a subtle citrus flavor.

SERVES 4

PREPARATION + COOKING
15 + 20 minutes + chilling

STORAGE
Keep in the fridge for 2 days.

SERVE THIS WITH...
Tomato Chutney (see page 105)
salad or steamed vegetables
Chunky Breadsticks (see page 87)
Apricot-Oat Slices (see page 80)
fresh fruit

HEALTH BENEFITS
Lima beans, like other beans and lentils, are packed with nutrients, fiber and protein—a combination that can help to stabilize blood sugar levels. Being a useful source of iron, they can help to avoid anemia and fatigue. They are also a good source of the minerals manganese, zinc and magnesium, which are essential co-factors in a number of enzymes that are important in energy production.

14 ounces canned lima beans, drained and rinsed
1 small zucchini, finely grated
scant ⅔ cup grated Cheddar cheese
1 tablespoon tahini

3 eggs
light olive oil, for greasing
¼ cup sesame seeds
3 cups fine wholewheat bread crumbs
1 tablespoon sumac

1 Put the lima beans in a food processor and blitz until smooth. Add the zucchini, cheese, tahini and one of the eggs, and pulse to combine. Scrape the bean mixture into a container, cover and chill for 30 minutes to firm up.
2 Preheat the oven to 425°F. Lightly grease a baking sheet and line it with parchment paper.
3 Mix the sesame seeds, bread crumbs and sumac together on a plate. Beat the remaining eggs in a bowl.
4 With damp hands, take 1 tablespoon of the mixture and roll into a walnut-size ball. Roll in the bread crumbs to coat, dip in the egg, then coat again in the bread crumbs. Repeat to make 12 balls. Put on the prepared baking sheet and bake until golden and crisp, about 20 minutes.

fig & goat cheese bruschetta

This imaginative variation of a toasted cheese sandwich mixes dried figs with creamy cheese.

8 moist, dried figs
2 tablespoons balsamic vinegar
2 teaspoons raw cane sugar
   or xylitol
2 ounces soft, mild goat
   cheese

8 slices of bread, such
   as rye, wholewheat or
   pumpernickel,
   about ½ inch thick
light olive oil, for brushing
freshly ground black pepper

1 Preheat the oven to 350°F.

2 Combine the figs, vinegar, sugar and 4 tablespoons of water in a small pan. Bring to a boil, then simmer until syrupy, about 5 minutes. Let cool, then cut the figs into small pieces with scissors.

3 Put the goat cheese in a bowl and mash with a fork, then fold in the figs. Season with a little black pepper.

4 Spread the bread slices on a baking sheet and brush with olive oil. Bake until the bread begins to crisp, about 1 minute. Spread the goat cheese mixture over the bread. Return to the oven and bake until the cheese is warmed through and the edges of the bread are golden, 1 to 2 minutes. Let cool slightly before serving.

SERVES 4

PREPARATION + COOKING
15 + 8 minutes

STORAGE
Keep in the fridge for 2 days.

SERVE THIS WITH...
vegetable sticks
mixed salad
1 handful of berries or grapes
Lemon-Coconut Macaroons
   (see page 78)

HEALTH BENEFITS
Dried figs are great for the digestive system, being a good source of soluble fiber plus the enzyme ficin, which can be soothing for the digestive tract. A concentrated source of nutrients, including iron and calcium and natural sugars, they make a useful pick-me-up when energy levels are low.

041

stuffed tomatoes

SERVES 4

PREPARATION
15 minutes

STORAGE
Keep in the fridge for 1 day.

SERVE THIS WITH...
Squash Scones (see page 82)
mixed salald
Mango-Orange Crêpes
  (see page 131)

HEALTH BENEFITS
Tahini (sesame seed paste) is a
wonderful nutrient-rich food for
growing children, especially any
that lack a good appetite. Rich in
zinc (a deficiency that has been
linked to poor appetite), tahini is
also a useful vegetarian source of
protein, healthy omega fats and B
vitamins to support energy levels.

Creamy hummus spooned into cherry
tomatoes makes fun finger food, perfect for
little mouths. Using flaxseed oil in the hummus
is an easy way to boost your child's intake of
healthy essential omega-3 and -6 fats, too.

14 ounces canned chickpeas,
  drained and rinsed
2 tablespoons lemon juice
2 garlic cloves, minced
½ teaspoon ground cumin

3 tablespoons tahini
2 tablespoons flaxseed oil
8 vine-ripened cherry
  tomatoes, cut in half
½ teaspoon smoked paprika

1 To make the hummus, put the chickpeas, lemon juice,
garlic, cumin and tahini in a food processor and blitz until
smooth and creamy. Blend in the oil. If the mixture is too
stiff, add a little water to form a thick purée.
2 Scoop out the centers of the tomatoes and discard.
Spoon the hummus into the tomatoes. Dust with a little
paprika before serving.

creamy dips

Dips are great eaten with crudites and breadsticks. Babies love them.

RED PEPPER-ALMOND DIP
3 jarred, roasted red bell peppers in oil, drained
1 garlic clove, minced
⅔ cup almonds
pinch of smoked paprika
1 tablespoon sun-dried tomato paste
3 tablespoons flaxseed oil
2 teaspoons balsamic vinegar
1 teaspoon raw cane sugar or xylitol

CARAMELIZED ONION DIP
4 tablespoons light olive oil
2 red onions, thinly sliced
½ cup crème fraîche
1 tablespoon low-salt soy sauce
1 tablespoon tahini
½ cup Greek yogurt
salt and freshly ground black pepper

1 To make the red pepper-almond dip, put the peppers, garlic, almonds and paprika in a food processor and blitz to form a chunky paste. Add the remaining ingredients and blitz until smooth, adding salt and pepper to taste. Add a little more oil, if needed, to thin.

2 To make the caramelized onion dip, heat the oil in a frying pan and sauté the onions until caramelized, 10 to 15 minutes. Drain on paper towels. Mix with the remaining ingredients.

3 Spoon the dips into separate bowls.

SERVES 4

PREPARATION + COOKING
20 + 15 minutes

STORAGE
Keep in the fridge for 3 days.

SERVE THIS WITH...
a selection of vegetable sticks
Chunky Breadsticks
(see page 87)
Zucchini & Apple Cake
(see page 84)

HEALTH BENEFITS
Rich in healthy monounsaturated fat, vitamin E and antioxidants, almonds are a protective, nutrient-dense food that are perfect for building healthy children. They are particularly high in calcium, which, together with magnesium, is important for nerve and muscle function and strengthening bones and teeth. An excellent protein source too, almonds can help to keep appetites satisfied and energy levels high.

SNACKS

Mid-morning and mid-afternoon snacks are important for keeping children fueled and will help to balance their blood sugar level, enabling them to feel energized and alert. Instead of candy and sugary drinks, opt for a snack that combines protein with some slow-releasing carbohydrate. Snacks are also a great opportunity to sneak some more fruit and vegetables into your child's diet, and here you will find a range of fabulous sweet and savory ideas. Whether it's Chunky Breadsticks, Squash Scones or Pumpkin-Seed Buns, or sweet treats like Cranberry Biscotti, No-Bake Whoopie Pies, Apricot-Oat Slices or Lemon-Coconut Macaroons, you will be amazed at how healthy and delicious snacks can be.

peanut butter & coconut balls

MAKES 8

PREPARATION
10 minutes + chilling

STORAGE
Keep in the fridge for 3 to 4 days.

SERVE THIS WITH…
fresh fruit

HEALTH BENEFITS
Instead of ordinary honey or agave nectar, you could use manuka honey, which is a natural sweetener that may be beneficial when used occasionally and in small amounts. Being a natural antiseptic, it is useful for treating sore throats, coughs and colds. Also, being strongly anti-microbial, it can help to tackle viruses and has been used topically for wound-healing. Honey should not be given to children under the age of one.

Little power nuggets, these sweet bites will help to re-energize your child when blood sugar levels are falling. Great for a mid-afternoon pick-me-up and an easy way to sneak in some additional omega-3, too.

2 tablespoons natural crunchy
   peanut butter
1 tablespoon flaxseed oil
1 tablespoon honey or agave
   nectar
1 tablespoon ground flaxseed

⅔ cup rolled oats
1 to 2 tablespoons
   unsweetened cocoa powder,
   or raw cacao powder to taste
⅓ cup dried shredded coconut

1 Put the peanut butter, oil and honey in a bowl and mix to form a stiff paste. Add the flaxseed, oats and cocoa powder and, using your hands, bring the mixture together to form a firm, slightly sticky paste.
2 Spread the coconut on a plate. With slightly damp hands, roll the peanut butter mixture into walnut-size balls, then coat in the coconut. Refrigerate to firm up slightly, about 30 minutes.

almond-chocolate butter on apple wedges

A simple energizing snack that children will adore. Healthier than any bought versions, the almond-chocolate butter is also delicious spread on toast and oat crackers.

1 tablespoon olive oil or melted coconut oil
1 tablespoon raw cane sugar or xylitol
1 tablespoon honey or agave nectar
scant ¾ cup almond or other nut butter

2 tablespoons raw cacao powder or 1 tablespoon unsweetened cocoa powder
2 teaspoons vanilla extract
2 apples, cored and cut into wedges

1 Put the oil, sugar and honey in a small pan and heat gently until all the sugar has melted. Add the almond nut butter, cacao powder and vanilla, then take the pan off the heat. Beat the mixture well until it is thoroughly combined and smooth.

2 Pour into a container, cover and let cool to room temperature.

3 Spread a little of the almond-chocolate butter on the apple wedges to serve.

SERVES 4–6

PREPARATION + COOKING
10 + 5 minutes

STORAGE
Keep the almond-chocolate butter in the fridge for 1 week.

SERVE THIS WITH...
glass of milk or milk alternative

HEALTH BENEFITS
Solid at room temperature, coconut oil is one of the best fats to cook with, because it is one of the only oils that can be heated to high temperatures without being converted into trans fats. It is also a great energy-booster, being rich in medium-chain triglycerides, which, rather than being stored by the body, are converted via the liver into immediate energy.

045

cranberry biscotti

These cookies are sweetened with cranberries.

SERVES 4

PREPARATION + COOKING
20 + 45 minutes

STORAGE
Keep in an airtight container for
1 week.

SERVE THIS WITH...
fresh fruit

HEALTH BENEFITS
Cranberries are rich in the
antioxidants known as
proanthocyanidins, which
appear to help prevent urinary
tract infections by preventing
bacteria from attaching onto
the urinary tract lining. Similar
effects have been seen in other
parts of the body, too, making
cranberries useful for preventing
Helicobacter pylori infection in
the stomach and dental decay.
When buying dried cranberries,
choose those without added
sugars.

light olive oil, for greasing
scant ¼ cup raw cane sugar
  or xylitol
2 eggs
1 teaspoon vanilla extract
1¼ cups almonds
pinch of salt

2 teaspoons finely grated
  orange zest
½ teaspoon baking soda
2 tablespoons arrowroot or
  cornstarch
½ cup dried cranberries
¼ cup pistachio nuts

1 Preheat the oven to 350°F. Lightly grease a baking sheet
and line it with parchment paper.

2 Put the sugar, eggs and vanilla in a blender and blend
until smooth.

3 Put the almonds in a food processor and blitz to form
a very fine flour. Tip into a bowl and add the salt, orange
zest, baking soda and arrowroot. Stir in the egg mixture,
cranberries and nuts.

4 Shape the dough into 2 small log shapes and set them
on the prepared baking sheet. Bake until lightly golden,
about 30 minutes.

5 Let cool for 15 minutes, then cut into ¾-inch slices on
the diagonal. Spread the slices on the baking sheet and
return to the oven to bake until golden and crisp, 10 to
15 minutes. Let cool before serving.

almond linzer cookies

MAKES 12

These jam-filled cookies are gluten-free.

PREPARATION + COOKING
15 + 10 minutes

light olive oil, for greasing
1⅔ cups almonds
1⅓ cups rice flour, plus extra
    for dusting
pinch of salt
½ teaspoon xanthan gum

¾ stick plus 1 tablespoon butter
⅓ cup raw cane sugar or xylitol
2 teaspoons vanilla extract
¼ cup pure fruit strawberry
    or raspberry jam (no added
    sugar)

STORAGE
Keep in an airtight container for
1 week.

SERVE THIS WITH...
fresh vegetable juice or fruit
  smoothie

1 Preheat the oven to 350°F. Lightly grease a baking sheet and line it with parchment paper.

2 Put the almonds in a blender and blend to form a fine powder. Tip into a large bowl and add the rice flour, salt and xanthan gum.

3 Melt the butter and sugar in a small pan over low heat. Stir into the flour with the vanilla and bring the mixture together to form a dough. Roll out to ½-inch thickness between 2 sheets of parchment paper.

4 Using a 4-inch cookie cutter, cut out 12 rounds. Cut out a small heart or circle from the center of 6 of the rounds.

5 Lightly press your finger into the center of the complete circles to make an indentation, then fill with a little jam. Put the hollow circles on the top.

6 Spread on the baking sheet. Bake until golden, about 10 minutes. Cool 10 minutes, then move to a wire rack.

HEALTH BENEFITS
Despite popular belief, butter is actually a nourishing food for children, since it is a useful source of vitamins A and E to support immune health as well as vitamin D, which is vital for healthy bones. Organic butter is a particularly good source of conjugated linoleic acid (CLA), which aids the body's use of fat for energy. It also contains butyric acid, a short-chain fatty acid that has antifungal properties and provides an energy source for the cells lining the colon, reducing inflammation and ensuring a healthy digestive system.

*chocolate cupcakes

These gluten-free cupcakes have a surprise berry jam center.

HEALTH BENEFITS
Naturally sweet and bursting with vitamin C, strawberries are a popular fruit with children. They are also rich in soluble fiber, which is important for maintaining a healthy digestive system, and contain ellagic acid, which supports immune health. Finally, they are a good source of B vitamins, which are needed for a healthy nervous system, tackling stress and supporting energy levels.

½ cup coconut flour
¼ cup unsweetened cocoa
powder
½ teaspoon salt
1 teaspoon gluten-free baking
powder
1 teaspoon baking soda
5 eggs

heaped ½ cup raw cane sugar
or xylitol
½ cup olive oil
2 teaspoons vanilla extract
⅓ cup pure fruit strawberry jam
7 ounces dairy-free semi-sweet
chocolate
6 strawberries

MAKES 12

PREPARATION + COOKING
20 + 30 minutes + freezing

STORAGE
Keep in an airtight container
for 3 to 4 days or freeze for up
to 1 month.

SERVE THIS WITH...
fresh fruit

1 Preheat the oven to 350°F. Put 12 paper cases in a
12-cup muffin pan.

2 Put the coconut flour, cocoa powder, salt, baking
powder and baking soda in a bowl and mix well.

3 Put the eggs, sugar, oil and vanilla in a food processor
and blitz to mix. Gradually add the dry ingredients, blitzing
to form a smooth batter.

4 Put 1 tablespoon of batter into each paper case. Add
1 teaspoon of jam and cover with the rest of the batter.

5 Bake until golden brown and firm, 20 to 25 minutes. Let
the cupcakes cool in the pan for 10 minutes, then unmold
onto a wire rack.

6 Melt the chocolate in a heatproof bowl set over a pan of
simmering water, then drizzle it over the cakes. Decorate
each with a strawberry half.

048

lemon-coconut macaroons

These deliciously light, gluten-free cookies require few ingredients and minimal effort.

MAKES 14

PREPARATION + COOKING
20 + 15 minutes

STORAGE
Keep in an airtight container for 1 week.

SERVE THIS WITH...
fresh fruit

HEALTH BENEFITS
Xylitol is an ideal healthy sweetener to use in recipes. With 40% fewer calories than table sugar and a low glycemic index, it has minimal impact on blood glucose levels. This makes it perfect for keeping energy levels high through the day, avoiding dips that can affect concentration. Xylitol has also been shown to help maintain healthy teeth.

light olive oil, for greasing
1⅔ cups dried shredded coconut, plus extra for sprinkling
⅓ cup raw cane sugar or xylitol
finely grated zest of 1 lemon
1 tablespoon arrowroot or cornstarch
3 egg whites
¼ teaspoon salt

1 Preheat the oven to 350°F. Lightly grease a baking sheet and line it with parchment paper.
2 Put the coconut and sugar in a food processor and blitz to form fine crumbs. Tip into a bowl and mix in the lemon zest and arrowroot.
3 Put the egg whites and salt in a large mixing bowl and beat until stiff peaks form. Using a large metal spoon, fold the coconut mixture lightly into the egg whites until thoroughly combined.
4 Spoon tablespoonfuls of the mixture onto the prepared baking sheet, spreading out slightly, to form 14 rounds. Bake until lightly colored, 10 to 15 minutes.
5 Let cool on the baking sheet for 10 minutes before transferring to a wire rack to cool completely.

no-bake whoopie pies

Delicious cookies that don't need baking!

light olive oil, for greasing
scant 1¼ cups pecans
heaped ¾ cup cashew nuts
1 tablespoon ground flaxseed
3 tablespoons melted
    coconut oil
2 tablespoons raw cane sugar
    or xylitol
¼ cup unsweetened cocoa
    powder
⅔ cup pitted dates

pinch of salt
finely grated zest of 1 lemon

FILLING
1 tablespoon cashew or other
    nut butter
finely grated zest of 2 lemons
juice of 1 lemon
⅓ cup melted coconut oil
3 tablespoons raw cane sugar
    or xylitol

MAKES 8

PREPARATION
20 minutes + chilling

STORAGE
Keep in the fridge for 1 week
or freeze for up to 1 month.

SERVE THIS WITH…
slices of fresh fruit

HEALTH BENEFITS
Pecans are rich in
monounsaturated fats and
antioxidants, particularly
vitamin E, which helps to lower
inflammation in the body and
protect against chronic diseases.
They also contain a range of
minerals, including calcium
and magnesium, which have a
calming effect on the body as
well as supporting bone health.

1 Lightly grease two 8-cup whoopie pie pans.

2 Put the nuts in a food processor and blitz to form fine crumbs. Pour into a bowl and stir in the ground flaxseed.

3 Blitz the remaining cookie ingredients to create a thick paste. Add the nuts and pulse to combine. Add 1 tablespoon of water to help bind the mixture.

4 Roll into 16 walnut-size pieces and press into the cups. Freeze until hard, about 30 minutes.

5 To make the filling, put all the ingredients in a blender and blend until smooth. Chill for 15 minutes.

6 Remove the cookies from the pan and sandwich pairs together with the filling.

MAKES 12

apricot-oat slices

Moist oaty bar cookies with an apricot filling.

STORAGE
Keep in the fridge for 1 week
or freeze for up to 1 month.

light olive oil, for greasing
2¼ cups moist dried apricots
½ cup orange juice
1 cup cashew nuts

2⅓ cups rolled oats
⅔ cup chopped pitted dates
1 tablespoon vanilla extract
scant ⅔ cup melted coconut oil

SERVE THIS WITH...
plain yogurt
slices of fresh apricot

HEALTH BENEFITS
Orange juice is an excellent
hydrator and energizer,
rich in immune-supporting
bioflavonoids and vitamin C.
Oranges also contain the citrus
oil known as limonene, which
is known for its anticancer and
disease-fighting properties.

1 Preheat the oven to 375°F. Grease an 8-inch square shallow
baking pan and line with parchment paper.
2 Put the apricots and orange juice in a small pan and simmer
gently until the apricots are very soft and most of the liquid
has been absorbed, about 5 minutes. Let cool slightly, then
blend using a hand blender to form a thick purée.
3 Put the cashew nuts in a food processor and blitz to form
a fine flour. Add the oats and pulse briefly to break them down.
Tip the mixture into a large bowl.
4 Put the dates, vanilla and melted coconut oil in the food
processor and blitz to form a paste. Add to the dry ingredients
and mix well with your hands to form a crumbly dough.
5 Spoon half of the dough into the prepared pan and press
down well with the back of a metal spoon. Spread the apricot
purée over it, then top with the remaining dough. Bake until
golden, 25 to 30 minutes. Let cool before cutting into bars.

choc-nut lemon bars

Packed with protein from the nuts and seeds and low in sugar, these gluten-free bars are full of energizing nutrients and slow-releasing carbs.

light olive oil, for greasing
finely grated zest and juice of
   3 lemons
⅔ cup pitted dates, plus
   scant ⅓ cup chopped dates
¼ cup raw cane sugar or xylitol
3 tablespoons walnut or other
   nut butter
scant 1¼ cups cashew nuts
1 cup walnuts
3 tablespoons sunflower seeds

scant 1¼ cups gluten-free rolled
   oats or buckwheat flakes
½ cup dried shredded coconut

FROSTING
7 ounces dairy-free semi-sweet
   chocolate
2 tablespoons raw cane sugar
   or xylitol
2 tablespoons walnut or other
   nut butter

1 Grease and line a 12- x 8-inch shallow baking pan.

2 Put the lemon zest and juice, whole dates, sugar and walnut butter in a blender and blend to form a smooth purée.

3 Put the nuts in a food processor and blitz to form a flour. Tip into a large bowl. Add the remaining ingredients and the date purée and mix thoroughly. Spoon into the prepared pan and press down firmly. Refrigerate for 1 hour.

4 To make the frosting, melt the chocolate, sugar and walnut butter in a pan. Pour the frosting over the cookie base and spread thinly. Refrigerate for 1 hour to harden. Cut into bars.

MAKES 18

PREPARATION
20 minutes + chilling

STORAGE
Keep in the fridge for 1 week or freeze for up to 1 month.

SERVE THIS WITH...
fresh fruit yogurt smoothie

HEALTH BENEFITS
Power-packed sunflower seeds are rich in minerals such as zinc, manganese, magnesium and iron, as well as B vitamins to support energy levels. They are also a good source of vitamin E—an antioxidant that keeps skin healthy and prevents damage caused by toxins.

squash scones

HEALTH BENEFITS
Butternut squash is rich in carotenoids, including lutein and zeaxanthin, which are essential nutrients for ensuring healthy eyesight. It is also a rich source of beta-carotene, the precursor for vitamin A, which supports the immune system and mucosal health, so useful for respiratory conditions. Squash is also rich in soluble fiber, which helps the digestive system to function smoothly. Finally, it is a good source of vitamin B6 and folate —important for the production of neurotransmitters in the brain and maintaining a healthy nervous system.

Moist and nourishing, these lovely little scones are filled with mashed butternut squash and mozzarella, making them an easy way to sneak a nutritious vegetable into your baby or toddler's meal. They are best served warm from the oven spread with a little butter or almond nut butter.

light olive oil, for greasing
9 ounces butternut squash, diced
2 cups self-rising wholewheat flour
1 tablespoon baking powder
1 teaspoon raw cane sugar or xylitol
4 tablespoons chilled butter, diced
⅓ cup shredded mozzarella cheese
1 egg, beaten
milk, for glazing
2 tablespoons grated Parmesan cheese

MAKES 8

PREPARATION + COOKING
20 + 35 minutes

SERVE THIS WITH...
soup or Creamy Dips (see page 69)

1 Preheat the oven to 400°F. Lightly grease a baking sheet.
2 Put the squash in a steamer and steam until tender, about 15 minutes. Transfer to a bowl and mash until smooth.
3 Put the flour, baking powder and sugar in a bowl. Rub in the butter with your fingertips until the mixture forms fine crumbs. Stir in the squash and mozzarella. Add the egg and knead to form a soft dough.
4 Turn out onto a lightly floured worktop and knead gently. Press out the dough to 1-inch thickness and use a 4-inch cookie cutter to cut out 8 rounds.
5 Spread the scones on the prepared baking sheet and brush with a little milk. Sprinkle with the Parmesan.
6 Bake until golden, about 20 minutes. Serve warm.

zucchini & apple cake

SERVES 12

PREPARATION + COOKING
20 + 45 minutes

STORAGE
Keep in the fridge for 3 to 4 days
or freeze for up to 1 month.

SERVE THIS WITH...
glass of milk or milk alternative

HEALTH BENEFITS
Zucchini have a high water
content, which, together with
their soluble fiber, makes them
useful for treating constipation.
They are also a good source of B
vitamins, including folate, which
is important for cell division
and DNA synthesis. The golden
varieties of summer squashes
are also rich in eye-supporting
carotenes lutein and zeaxanthin.

This delicious moist cake, which is gluten-free,
combines chocolate with zucchini and apple. For
an extra treat, you could drizzle melted chocolate
over the top.

4 eggs
heaped ½ cup raw cane sugar
   or xylitol
1 teaspoon vanilla extract
pinch of salt
scant 2 cups grated zucchini
2 apples, grated

2 cups ground almonds
scant 1 cup rice flour
⅓ cup unsweetened cocoa powder
1 tablespoon gluten-free baking
   powder
1½ cups dairy-free semi-sweet
   chocolate chips

1 Preheat the oven to 350°F. Lightly grease an 8-inch cake pan
or 9- x 5- x 3-inch loaf pan and line it with parchment paper.
2 Put the eggs, sugar, vanilla and salt in a bowl and beat
together. Stir in the zucchini and apples.
3 In a separate bowl, mix together the remaining ingredients.
Add the zucchini mixture and stir to combine. Spoon the batter
into the prepared pan.
4 Bake until firm, 35 to 45 minutes. Let cool in the pan for
5 minutes, then unmold onto a wire rack to cool completely.

pumpkin-seed buns

Little buns filled with pesto and grated cheese.

light olive oil, for greasing
1 cup self-rising wholewheat flour,
    plus extra for dusting
1¼ cups white bread flour
2 teaspoons raw cane sugar
    or xylitol
1 teaspoon baking powder
2 tablespoons butter, chilled
scant ⅔ cup lowfat (2%) milk
1 cup grated Cheddar cheese
beaten egg, for glazing

PUMPKIN-SEED PESTO
¼ cup pumpkin-seed butter
¼ cup pumpkin seeds
⅔ cup basil leaves
1 garlic clove, minced
1 teaspoon lemon juice
2 tablespoons light olive oil
2 tablespoons grated Parmesan
    cheese

MAKES 12

PREPARATION + COOKING
20 + 35 minutes

STORAGE
Keep in an airtight container for
2 days or freeze for up to 1 month.

SERVE THIS WITH...
homemade soup
vegetable sticks

HEALTH BENEFITS
Basil is a well-known anti-
inflammatory herb that may be
beneficial for conditions such as
irritable bowel, inflammatory bowel
and asthma. It is also anti-bacterial,
so particularly useful if your child
suffers with digestive upsets. Fresh
herbs are more potent than dried
and a great way to season dishes
without the need for salt.

1 Preheat the oven to 400°F. Lightly grease an 8-inch round shallow cake pan.
2 Put the flours, sugar and baking powder in a bowl. Rub in the butter, then stir in the milk and mix to form a soft dough.
3 Knead the dough on a lightly floured worktop until smooth. Roll out to a large rectangle about ¾ inch thick.
4 Blitz the pesto ingredients in a food processor until coarse-fine. Spread over the dough. Sprinkle with the Cheddar.
5 Starting from a long side, roll up the dough like a jelly roll. Cut across into 12 slices. Arrange in the pan in a single layer so they are touching each other. Brush with the beaten egg.
6 Bake until golden brown, 30 to 35 minutes. Serve warm.

teriyaki mixed seeds

SERVES 10–12

PREPARATION + COOKING
5 + 5 minutes

STORAGE
Keep in the fridge for 3 to 4 days.

SERVE THIS WITH...
fresh or dried fruit

HEALTH BENEFITS
Toasted seeds are a wonderful alternative snack to chips and other processed savory nibbles, like roasted peanuts, which are often high in saturated fats, trans fats and additives as well as added sugar and salt. Protein-rich seeds are a perfect choice to satisfy your child's appetite and keep them energized in between meals.

SERVES 10–12

Seeds are a great source of essential omega-3 and -6 fatty acids and also contain plenty of protein, vitamins and minerals—all vital for growing children. A handful of seeds makes the perfect energizing snack. To make them more appealing to children, toast them with this simple Japanese-style sauce. Make a batch of them and store in an airtight container in the fridge.

heaped ¾ cup sunflower seeds
heaped ¾ cup pumpkin seeds
1 tablespoon low-salt soy sauce
1 tablespoon mirin

pinch of raw cane sugar
  or xylitol

1 Put the seeds in a frying pan and toast them gently for 2 to 3 minutes, stirring.
2 Pour the soy sauce, mirin and sugar over the seeds and stir to coat all of them. Keep stirring for a couple of minutes until the seeds are dry and golden brown.
3 Let cool before serving.

chunky breadsticks

Breadsticks are popular with children of all ages.

1⅓ cups wholewheat bread flour
2 cups white bread flour
½-ounce quick-rising active
   dry yeast
½ teaspoon honey
pinch of salt

scant ½ cup light olive oil, plus
   extra for greasing and brushing
6 garlic cloves, minced
1 tablespoon balsamic vinegar
1 teaspoon raw cane sugar
   or xylitol
2 tablespoons sesame seeds

MAKES 8–10

PREPARATION + COOKING
20 + 25 minutes + rising

STORAGE
Keep in an airtight container for
4 to 5 days.

SERVE THIS WITH…
soup or Creamy Dips (see page 69)

HEALTH BENEFITS
Olive oil is rich in monounsaturated
fatty acids and antioxidants,
including phenols, which have been
shown to help lower inflammation
in the body, making it useful for
treating conditions such as asthma
and eczema.

1 Put the flours, yeast, honey and salt in a large bowl. Pour in 5 tablespoons of the oil and 1 cup warm water and mix with a wooden spoon to form a soft, springy dough.

2 Knead on a floured worktop for 5 minutes. Put in an oiled bowl, cover with plastic wrap and let rise for 1 hour.

3 Preheat the oven to 400°F. Grease a baking sheet.

4 Heat the remaining 2 tablespoons oil in a small pan and sauté the garlic until soft. Add the balsamic vinegar, sugar and 2 tablespoons water and cook gently for 1 minute.

5 Roll out the dough to form a large rectangle. Spread the garlic mixture over half of the dough and sprinkle with the seeds. Fold the dough over in half and press down to seal.

6 Cut the dough into long strips and roll each to form a stick, then twist. Put on the baking sheet and brush with a little oil.

7 Bake until golden brown, about 20 minutes. Let cool.

DINNERS

Sharing a meal with your child is one of the best ways to encourage healthy eating, as well as spending family time together. While all the recipes in this chapter can be eaten as finger foods, they can also be incorporated into main meals and are perfect for the whole family. There is a whole range of dishes to suit every taste, even for vegetarian or faddy eaters. All the dishes are packed with healthy ingredients, protein, vitamins and minerals to support your child's growth and development. They have also been designed with our busy lifestyles in mind—simple and quick to prepare, so there is no need to spend ages in the kitchen.

chicken kiev patties

All the traditional garlic flavors, but smaller.

SERVES 4

PREPARATION + COOKING
15 + 25 minutes

STORAGE
Keep in the fridge for 2 days.

SERVE THIS WITH...
mixed salad
sweet potato wedges baked
  in olive oil
Ice-Cream Sandwiches
  (see page 126)

HEALTH BENEFITS
Chicken is a popular meat with
children, providing plenty of
protein for the growth and repair
of body cells while being low in
saturated fat. It is a useful source
of the mineral selenium, which
can often be low in people's
diets yet is essential for a
healthy immune system. Choose
organic or free-range chicken, if
possible, as these are generally
leaner and contain a greater
proportion of essential omega-3
and -6 fats.

light olive oil, for greasing
9 ounces skinless, boneless
  chicken breast, chopped
2 garlic cloves, minced
¼ cup herb- or garlic-and-herb-
  flavored cream cheese
1 handful of parsley

heaped ⅓ cup all-purpose flour
1½ cups dry bread crumbs
3 tablespoons grated Parmesan
  cheese
2 eggs, beaten
freshly ground black pepper

1 Preheat the oven to 400°F. Lightly grease a baking sheet
and line it with parchment paper.
2 Put the chicken, garlic, cream cheese, parsley and some
pepper in a food processor and blitz to form a chunky
paste. Shape into 8 patties.
3 Put the flour on a plate, the bread crumbs and
Parmesan together on another plate and the eggs in a
shallow bowl.
4 Dust the patties with flour, dip into the egg and, finally,
coat with the Parmesan crumbs. Place on the baking
sheet and bake until crisp, 20 to 25 minutes.

chicken wings with chili-tomato sauce

This is a healthy and delicious baked alternative to fast-food chicken pieces.

4 chicken wings
light olive oil, for greasing

CHILI-TOMATO SAUCE
2 cups tomato purée
2 tablespoons Worcestershire sauce

2 tablespoons raw cane sugar or xylitol
1 tablespoon Dijon mustard
1 red chili (mildly hot or hot, to taste), seeded and minced
1 garlic clove, minced

SERVES 4

PREPARATION + COOKING
15 + 45 minutes + marinating

STORAGE
Keep in the fridge for 2 days.

SERVE THIS WITH...
coleslaw
vegetable sticks
Banana Choc–Nut Bites
(see page 134)

HEALTH BENEFITS
Tomato purée and canned tomatoes are rich in carotenoids, including beta-carotene, which is necessary for the production of vitamin A. This is a vital nutrient for a healthy immune system and the maintenance of a healthy mucosal membrane—important for skin, respiratory and digestive health.

1 Put all the ingredients for the chili-tomato sauce in a small pan. Bring to a boil, then simmer until slightly thickened, about 10 minutes. Cool to room temperature.
2 Trim the end off each chicken wing, then cut each in half through the joint. Put in a bowl and coat with a little of the sauce. Let marinate in the fridge for 1 to 2 hours. Put the remaining sauce in a bowl, cover and refrigerate.
3 Preheat the oven to 400°F. Put the chicken in a single layer on a greased rack in a roasting pan. Bake until golden and cooked (the juices should run clear when the thickest part is pierced with a skewer), about 30 minutes.
4 Serve the chicken wings with the remaining sauce.

crisp drumsticks

This is a tasty "Southern fried"-style dish.

SERVES 4

PREPARATION + COOKING
20 + 30 minutes

STORAGE
Keep the chicken in the fridge for 2 days and the sauce for 3 to 4 days.

SERVE THIS WITH
Chili-Tomato Sauce (see page 91)
roasted vegetables and potatoes
mixed salad
Grilled Pineapple (see page 130)

HEALTH BENEFITS
These crisp chicken bites are baked with a minimum of fat, making them a healthy option for children. Most chicken finger food at fast-food restaurants is deep-fried, which increases our intake of saturated fats as well as trans fats, which have been shown to be harmful to our health.

light olive oil, for greasing
8 small chicken drumsticks
heaped ⅓ cup all-purpose flour
3 eggs, beaten
2 cups dry bread crumbs
1 teaspoon cayenne pepper
1 teaspoon dried thyme
1 teaspoon dried oregano
freshly ground black pepper

1 Preheat the oven to 400°F. Lightly grease a baking sheet and line it with parchment paper.

2 Remove the skin from the drumsticks and score the meat lightly with a sharp knife.

3 Put the flour on a plate and season with black pepper. Put the beaten eggs in a shallow dish. Mix together the bread crumbs, cayenne and herbs on another plate.

4 Coat the chicken in the flour and shake off the excess. Dip in the egg, then coat thoroughly in the crumbs.

5 Put the chicken in a single layer on the prepared baking sheet and bake until cooked through (the juices should run clear when the chicken is pierced in the thickest part with a skewer), 25 to 30 minutes. Turn them over halfway through cooking to ensure they are golden all over.

6 Serve with a dipping sauce of your choice.

pomegranate-glazed chicken thighs

Sweet and sticky, these delicious chicken pieces are coated with a tangy Middle-Eastern marinade made using pomegranate molasses.

4 skinless, boneless chicken
   thighs, cut in half
2 tablespoons pomegranate
   molasses

2 garlic cloves, minced
pinch of ground cinnamon
light olive oil, for greasing
freshly ground black pepper

1 Put the chicken thighs in a shallow container.
2 Mix together the pomegranate molasses, garlic and cinnamon in a bowl, and season with black pepper. Rub the mixture all over the chicken. Cover and let marinate in the fridge for a few hours or overnight.
3 Preheat the broiler. Lightly grease a baking sheet.
4 Put the chicken thighs on the prepared baking sheet. Broil, 5 to 6 inches from the heat, until cooked through (the juices should run clear when the chicken is pierced in the thickest part with a skewer), about 15 minutes. Brush with any remaining marinade during cooking and turn to make sure the thighs are glazed all over.

SERVES 4

PREPARATION + COOKING
10 + 15 minutes + marinating

STORAGE
Keep in the fridge for 1 day.

SERVE THIS WITH...
steamed green beans and
   snow peas
corn on the cob
Apricot-Oat Slices (see page 80)
fresh fruit

HEALTH BENEFITS
Garlic is a natural antibiotic and is antimicrobial, making it useful for protecting your child against infections including parasites and bacterial and yeast infections. It is also rich in sulfurous compounds that support liver detoxification and immune function. Being anti-inflammatory, it may also protect against asthma.

spicy chicken kebabs

A variation on a traditional Turkish shish kebab.

SERVES 4

PREPARATION + COOKING
15 + 15 minutes + marinating

STORAGE
Keep the kebabs in the fridge
for 1 day and the sauce for
2 to 3 days.

SERVE THIS WITH...
4 mini wholewheat pita breads
shredded lettuce
sliced tomatoes
Summer Berry Ice Cups
(see page 125)

HEALTH BENEFITS
Flaxseed oil is rich in the
essential omega-3 fatty acids
and is a useful way of increasing
your child's intake, especially
for vegetarians. Omega-3
fats are crucial for cognitive
function because they form an
essential part of the membrane
of brain cells, important for
communication within and
between cells, aiding brain
function.

9 ounces skinless,
  boneless chicken breast,
  cut into cubes
8 cherry tomatoes

MARINADE
3 garlic cloves, minced
1 tablespoon sun-dried tomato
  paste
¼ cup plain yogurt
2 tablespoons lemon juice
½ teaspoon salt
½ teaspoon raw cane sugar
  or xylitol

1 teaspoon smoked paprika
1 teaspoon grated lemon zest

SAUCE
⅔ cup plain yogurt
¼ cup tahini
½ teaspoon ground cumin
juice of ½ lemon
1 tablespoon chopped mint
1 teaspoon flaxseed oil
1 garlic clove, minced

1 Put the chicken in a shallow container. Mix the marinade
ingredients together and pour over the chicken. Cover and
let marinate in the fridge for 1 hour or overnight.
2 Put all the sauce ingredients in a bowl and mix well.
3 Soak 4 wooden skewers in water for 30 minutes.
Preheat the broiler. Thread the chicken and tomatoes onto
the skewers. Broil, 5 to 6 inches from the heat, turning
occasionally, until golden and cooked, 10 to 15 minutes.
4 Let cool slightly. Remove the skewers before serving
the chicken with the sauce.

thai-spiced turkey balls

Little balls of turkey packed with Thai flavors.

light olive oil, for greasing
7 ounces ground turkey
1 lime leaf, shredded
1 lemongrass stalk, minced
2 teaspoons cornstarch
4 scallions, minced
freshly ground black pepper

DUNKING BROTH
2 shallots, minced
1 red chili, seeded and minced
2 teaspoons raw cane sugar
    or xylitol
1 tablespoon Thai fish sauce
¾-inch piece fresh gingerroot,
    peeled and grated
1¼ cups fresh chicken stock

1 Preheat the oven to 400°F. Lightly grease a baking sheet and line it with parchment paper.
2 To make the meatballs, mix all the ingredients together in a large bowl. Season with a little black pepper.
3 With damp hands, shape the mixture into 12 balls and put them on the baking sheet. Bake, turning twice, until cooked and golden brown all over, 20 to 25 minutes.
4 Meanwhile, bring the broth ingredients to a boil in a pan and simmer for 10 minutes. Dunk the balls in the broth.

SERVES 4

PREPARATION + COOKING
15 + 25 minutes

STORAGE
Keep the meatballs and broth in the fridge for 2 days.

SERVE THIS WITH...
rice noodles
snow peas and baby corn
Mango Ice Pops (see page 124)

HEALTH BENEFITS
Turkey is a fantastic lowfat, protein-rich food, often reserved for festive occasions only. It is a good source of zinc—an essential mineral component of over 200 enzymes in the body, essential for growth, a healthy nervous system and brain development. It is also rich in B vitamins. All B vitamins are crucial for mental health, and, being water-soluble, they pass rapidly out of the body, so your child needs a regular intake daily.

asian-spiced duck

Strips of lean duck breast in a sweet, fragrant sauce are delicious and packed with protein.

SERVES 4

PREPARATION + COOKING
15 + 25 minutes + marinating

STORAGE
Keep in the fridge for 2 days.

SERVE THIS WITH
8 mandarin pancakes
strips of cucumber
shredded lettuce
hoisin sauce or tamari soy sauce
Sweet Cherry Samosas
   (see page 132)

HEALTH BENEFITS
Although honey is an intense
sweetener, it does possess some
health benefits, particularly if it
is unprocessed organic honey.
Rich in antioxidants, honey is
a natural antiseptic and useful
for coughs, colds and digestive
upsets. Use in small amounts
only and do not feed to children
under one year old.

2 duck breasts, about 9 ounces
   total weight
2 tablespoons honey or agave
   nectar
1 teaspoon five-spice powder
1 garlic clove, minced

2 star anise
3 tablespoons soy sauce
⅔ cup low-sodium chicken
   stock
2 tablespoons Chinese rice
   wine

1 Put the duck breasts in a bowl. Drizzle the honey over and sprinkle with the five-spice powder.
2 Put the remaining ingredients in a small pan and bring to a boil. Lower the heat and simmer until syrupy, about 5 minutes. Let cool to room temperature.
3 Prick the duck breasts with a fork and pour the stock mixture over them. Let marinate in the fridge for at least 15 minutes.
4 Preheat the oven to 375°F.
5 Put the duck breasts on a rack in a roasting pan and roast until golden and cooked through, about 20 minutes. Let the duck rest for 10 minutes, then shred into thin strips to use as a filling for mandarin pancakes.

crisp pork bites

A great finger-food alternative to a Sunday roast.

2¼ pounds boneless fresh pork
   belly (side pork)
1 teaspoon five-spice powder
4 cups low-sodium chicken
   stock

2 garlic cloves, minced
1 cup apple juice
2 tablespoons light olive oil
freshly ground black pepper

1 Preheat the oven to 350°F.

2 Rub the meat side of the pork belly with the five-spice powder and season with a little black pepper.

3 Put the chicken stock, garlic and apple cider in a stovetop-to-oven casserole large enough to accommodate the pork. Bring to a boil, then lower the heat to a simmer and add the pork. It should be submerged, so add a little water if needed. Cover and cook in the oven for 3 hours.

4 Let the pork cool in the stock, then transfer to a tray and refrigerate for 1 hour. Discard the stock.

5 Cut the pork into bite-size squares. Heat the oil in a large frying pan. Add the pork, skin-side down, and cook until the skin is crisp, about 5 minutes. Turn over and cook the meat side until brown, 2 to 3 minutes. Repeat until all the pork is cooked (probably 3 batches).

6 Drain on paper towels and serve hot or cold.

SERVES 8

PREPARATION + COOKING
15 minutes + 3 hours 30 minutes
+ cooling + chilling

STORAGE
Keep in the fridge for 2 days.

SERVE THIS WITH…
apple sauce
sweet potato wedges
steamed vegetable florets
Apple & Pecan Tarts
  (see page 139)

HEALTH BENEFITS
Pork is a great protein food, rich in a whole range of vitamins and minerals, including selenium, zinc, iron and magnesium, which are important for energy production and immune health. It also contains a wealth of B vitamins, which are vital for healthy brain function and tackling stress and anxiety.

pork satay sticks

Lean strips of pork coated in a creamy almond sauce create a delicious dish.

MAKES 8

PREPARATION + COOKING
15 + 25 minutes

STORAGE
Keep in the fridge for 1 day.

SERVE THIS WITH...
steamed rice
wilted greens
Grilled Pineapple (see page 130)
plain yogurt

HEALTH BENEFITS
Coconut cream provides plenty of lauric acid—the same fatty acid that is found in breast milk and is known for its antiviral and antibacterial properties

scant ¾ cup almond nut butter or other nut butter
generous ¾ cup canned coconut cream
3 tablespoons sweet chili sauce
1 garlic clove, minced
½ cup low-sodium chicken stock
1 tablespoon lemon juice
1 pound lean pork tenderloin, cut into long strips
1 tablespoon minced cilantro
freshly ground black pepper

1 Soak 8 wooden skewers in cold water for at least 30 minutes. Meanwhile, preheat the oven to 350°F.
2 Put the almond butter, coconut cream, chili sauce, garlic, stock and lemon juice in a small pan and bring to a boil. Reduce the heat and simmer until the sauce thickens slightly, 1 to 2 minutes. Let cool for 5 minutes.
3 Thread the pork strips onto the soaked skewers and put them in a large, shallow baking dish. Pour half of the satay sauce over them. Bake until cooked through, about 20 minutes.
4 Put the remaining satay sauce in a small bowl, season with black pepper and sprinkle with the cilantro. Remove the sticks before serving the pork with the sauce.

herby koftas

This is a quick and easy kofta recipe that can be prepared ahead and kept chilled until required. The pine nuts provide texture and additional minerals to the dish. This is a great energy booster, rich in protein, B vitamins and iron.

1 pound lean ground lamb
1 egg, beaten
½ teaspoon ground cumin
2 tablespoons minced mint
1 tablespoon minced parsley

¼ cup pine nuts, minced
1 garlic clove, minced
1 red onion, grated
light olive oil, for greasing

1 Soak 12 skewers in cold water for at least 30 minutes.
2 Meanwhile, put all the ingredients in a bowl and mix together with your hands. Form into 12 balls, then mold each ball around the end of a skewer to form a little sausage shape. Put on a tray and refrigerate for 30 minutes to firm up.
3 Preheat the broiler. Lightly grease a baking sheet.
4 Transfer the skewers to the prepared baking sheet and broil, 5 to 6 inches from the heat, turning frequently, until the lamb is browned all over and cooked through, 10 to 15 minutes. Remove from the skewers before serving.

SERVES 6

PREPARATION + COOKING
15 + 15 minutes + chilling

STORAGE
Keep in the fridge for 1 day.

SERVE THIS WITH...
Greek yogurt
wholewheat pita breads
sliced lettuce and tomatoes

HEALTH BENEFITS
Pine nuts are incredibly rich in protein, making them useful for satisfying appetites and balancing blood sugar. They are also high in healthy monounsaturated fats, which can help to lower inflammation in the body. Packed with iron (a key component of hemoglobin, the oxygen-carrying pigment in blood that supplies energy), they are a great energizing food. They also supply plenty of magnesium, which helps to alleviate muscle cramps, tension and fatigue.

067

greek lamb patties

MAKES 12

PREPARATION + COOKING
15 + 25 minutes

STORAGE
Keep the patties in the fridge
for 2 days and the sauce for
3 to 4 days.

SERVE THIS WITH...
mini pita breads
vegetable sticks

HEALTH BENEFITS
Feta cheese contains less fat than
many cheeses and has a mild
flavor that will appeal to children.
It is a great way of adding
more protein to dishes as well
as providing bone-supporting
calcium. Traditionally, feta was
made with sheep milk. If you
can't find sheep milk or goat
milk versions, choose one made
from organic cow milk to avoid
antibiotic residues. It is high in
salt, so use sparingly and do not
add salt to the recipe.

These little meat patties make perfect finger
food for children. Ideal for parties or for
toddlers who are always on the go, the patties
are packed with nutritious ingredients.

light olive oil, for greasing
9 ounces ground lean lamb
1 garlic clove, minced
1 tablespoon tomato paste
¼ cup chopped pitted black
   olives
heaped ⅓ cup crumbled
   feta cheese
½ teaspoon ground cumin

½ cup soft wholewheat
   bread crumbs
freshly ground black pepper

YOGURT SAUCE
⅔ cup Greek yogurt
1 handful of mint leaves,
   minced
1 garlic clove, minced

1 Preheat the oven to 400°F. Lightly grease a baking sheet
and line it with parchment paper.
2 Put all the ingredients for the patties in a large bowl
and mix together until thoroughly combined. With damp
hands, shape the mixture into 12 little patties.
3 Put them on the prepared baking sheet and bake until
brown and cooked through, 20 to 25 minutes.
4 Meanwhile, put the ingredients for the yogurt sauce in
a bowl and stir well. Cover and refrigerate until needed.
5 Serve the lamb patties hot, with the yogurt sauce
drizzled over.

pesto & lamb frittatas

These tasty little bites are a great way to use up leftover roast lamb with lots of vegetables.

light olive oil, for greasing
8 asparagus spears
scant ¼ cup frozen peas
6 eggs, beaten
scant ⅔ cup heavy cream
1 zucchini, grated

2 tablespoons pesto
¼ cup grated Parmesan cheese
1 tablespoon snipped chives
scant ¼ cup diced roast lamb
freshly ground black pepper

1 Preheat the oven to 375°F. Lightly grease 8 cups in a muffin pan.
2 Bring a frying pan of water to a boil. Add the asparagus and blanch until just tender, 1 to 2 minutes. Drain, then cut into bite-size pieces.
3 Put the peas in a bowl. Pour boiling water over them and let stand for 2 to 3 minutes, then drain.
4 Put the eggs and cream in a bowl and whisk together, then stir in the remaining ingredients, including the asparagus and peas, and season with a little black pepper.
5 Spoon the mixture into the cups in the prepared muffin pan. Bake until golden and puffy, 20 to 25 minutes. Let cool for 5 to 10 minutes before unmolding.

SERVES 4

PREPARATION + COOKING
15 + 30 minutes

STORAGE
Keep in the fridge for 2 days.

SERVE THIS WITH...
steamed vegetables or mixed salad
Squash Scones (see page 82)
Ice-Cream Sandwiches
  (see page 126)
fresh fruit

HEALTH BENEFITS
Asparagus contains the amino acid asparagine, which is known to support detoxification and ease fluid retention, making it useful to help alleviate bloating as well as supporting liver and kidney function. It is also packed with folate—an essential B vitamin for the production of hormones and neurotransmitters in the brain. Asparagus is also rich in powerful antioxidants, including vitamins C, E and glutathione, to support immune health.

beet & beef mini burgers

MAKES 8

PREPARATION + COOKING
15 + 10 minutes + chilling

STORAGE
Keep in the fridge for 2 days.

SERVE THIS WITH...
wholewheat rolls or pita breads
mixed salad leaves
Tomato Chutney (see page 105)
Peaches with Berry Syrup
   (see page 128)

HEALTH BENEFITS
Beets are well known as a blood-boosting food, being rich in iron and folic acid to help build up red blood cells and prevent fatigue and anemia. They also contain nitrate, which the body uses to create nitric oxide—important for circulation and cardiovascular health. Folic acid can also help to lower levels of homocysteine, a toxic chemical that has been linked to a range of chronic conditions, including poor mental function.

Beets blend beautifully with lean ground beef to make wonderfully moist burgers that kids will love, making this another great way to sneak in extra vegetables.

1 pound ground steak
4 ounces cooked beets, grated
1 shallot, minced

light olive oil, for greasing
freshly ground black pepper

1 Put the beef, beets and shallot in a large bowl and season with black pepper. Mix together with your hands, then shape into 8 burgers. Put on a plate, cover and refrigerate for 30 minutes to firm up.

2 Lightly grease a ridged grill pan with oil, then heat. Grill the mini burgers, in batches, until well browned and done to your taste, 3 to 4 minutes per side. Serve hot.

meaty pasta slice

A delicious pasta bake cut into slices.

1 tablespoon light olive oil,
    plus extra for greasing
1 cup lean ground beef
1 small red onion, minced
1 carrot, peeled and grated
14 ounces canned crushed
    tomatoes

¾ cup wholewheat macaroni or
    other small pasta shapes
6 eggs, beaten
scant 1 cup grated Cheddar
    cheese
scant ⅔ cup grated Parmesan
    cheese

1 Preheat the oven to 350°F. Lightly grease a 9- x 12-inch
shallow baking dish.
2 Heat the oil in a large frying pan and fry the beef for
5 minutes, stirring occasionally. Add the onion and cook
for 2 to 3 minutes, then stir in the carrot and tomatoes
and bring to a boil. Simmer for 15 minutes, stirring
frequently; add a little water if too dry. Set aside.
3 Cook the pasta according to the directions on the
package, then drain. Add to the beef mixture.
4 Beat the eggs and Cheddar together in a bowl, then stir
into the beef mixture. Tip into the prepared baking dish
and sprinkle with the Parmesan. Bake until set and golden
brown on top, about 40 minutes. Cover with foil during
baking if the top gets too brown.
5 Let cool in the dish, then serve in slices.

SERVES 8–10

PREPARATION + COOKING
20 minutes + 1 hour 20 minutes

STORAGE
Keep in the fridge for 2 to
3 days.

SERVE THIS WITH…
mixed salad
Frozen Pineapple Cheesecake
    Slice (see page 138)

HEALTH BENEFITS
The quality of the meat you buy
will greatly influence the nutrient
content of your dish: Meat from
animals that have been reared
organically will tend to be leaner
and richer in nutrients. Ground
beef is a protein-packed food
that supplies plenty of iron, zinc
and B12. Zinc helps with cell
growth and improves immunity.
Vitamin B12 promotes the body's
production of red blood cells
and helps to keep the brain and
nervous system functioning at
their peak.

beef & mushroom potato cups

Little potatoes make the perfect base for this creamy mushroom filling.

SERVES 4

PREPARATION + COOKING
20 + 30 minutes

STORAGE
Keep in the fridge for 2 days.

SERVE THIS WITH...
coleslaw
vegetable sticks
fresh fruit and plain yogurt
Peanut Butter & Coconut Balls
   (see page 72)

HEALTH BENEFITS
New potatoes are a low glycemic carbohydrate, which means they release their sugars slowly into the bloodstream, so avoiding sudden highs and then lows in energy levels. If you eat the skin, you also increase the fiber content. Potatoes are also a good source of Vitamins C, B6 and potassium. B6 is vital for the production of neurotransmitters, including serotonin, which can help to boost our mood.

12 small to medium potatoes
1 tablespoon light olive oil,
   plus extra for greasing
6 button mushrooms, chopped
1 teaspoon wholegrain mustard
3 tablespoons Greek yogurt
¼ cup grated Gruyère cheese
2 slices of lean roast beef,
   minced
freshly ground black pepper

1 Put the whole potatoes in a steamer and cook until just tender, about 10 minutes. Drain and let cool.
2 Preheat the oven to 350°F. Grease a baking sheet.
3 Heat the oil in a pan and sauté the mushrooms until soft, 2 to 3 minutes.
4 Cut a thin slice lengthwise from the top of each potato. Using a teaspoon, carefully scoop out most of the flesh from inside. Put this into a bowl with the mustard, yogurt, cheese, mushrooms and beef, and mash together. Season to taste with black pepper.
5 Spoon the filling into the potato shells and set on the prepared baking sheet. Put any excess filling in a small dish. Bake until heated through, about 15 minutes.

coconut-salmon sticks with tomato chutney

A delicious, healthy version of fish sticks.

1 pound skinless salmon fillet,
   cut into bite-size strips
¼ cup cornstarch
2 eggs, lightly beaten
1¼ cups dried shredded
   coconut
⅓ cup sesame seeds
light olive oil, for greasing
freshly ground black pepper

TOMATO CHUTNEY
1¼ cups roughly chopped
   vine-ripened tomatoes
⅓ cup cider vinegar
⅓ cup raw cane sugar or xylitol
heaped ⅓ cup raisins
1 red chili (mildly hot or hot, to
   taste), seeded and minced
1 red onion, minced

1 To make the chutney, heat the tomatoes, vinegar and sugar in a pan over low heat, stirring until the sugar has dissolved. Add the remaining ingredients and simmer until thickened, about 20 minutes. Let cool.
2 Preheat the oven to 400°F.
3 Pat the salmon dry. Put the cornstarch on a plate and season with black pepper. Put the beaten eggs on another plate. Mix the coconut and sesame seeds on a third.
4 Working in batches, toss the salmon strips in the cornstarch, then egg, then coconut mixture. Transfer to a greased parchment-lined baking sheet. Bake until golden, about 20 minutes. Serve hot or cold with the chutney.

SERVES 4–6

PREPARATION + COOKING
15 + 45 minutes + chilling

STORAGE
Keep the fish in the fridge for 2 days and the chutney for 1 week.

SERVE THIS WITH...
peas and corn on the cob
mixed salad
Banana Choc-Nut Bites
   (see page 134)

HEALTH BENEFITS
Lycopene, a carotenoid and pigment that contributes to the red color of tomatoes, is a major contributor to this fruit's health-promoting power. It is also an important antioxidant for protecting the skin from UV damage, reducing the risk of cancers, and protecting cells and tissue from free radical damage. As it is fat-soluble, it needs a bit of fat to transport it into the bloodstream, so combining it with oily fish is perfect.

italian tuna balls

HEALTH BENEFITS
Canned tuna is an excellent, convenient protein-packed food for children. It also provides plenty of energy-boosting B vitamins, including B3 (niacin), which is important for balancing blood sugar levels, and selenium, for a healthy immune system. Canned tuna is not, however, a good source of omega-3 fats, because they are destroyed during the canning process.

A truly healthy alternative to fish nuggets and burgers, these nutritious little balls contain tinned tuna blended with ricotta cheese, basil and lemon zest to make a flavor-packed dish for children of all ages.

7 ounces canned tuna In ollve
oil, drained
2 cups soft wholewheat
bread crumbs
⅓ cup ricotta cheese
finely grated zest of 1 lemon
1 tablespoon minced basil
1 egg
freshly ground black pepper
all-purpose flour, for dusting

2 tablespoons olive oil or
coconut oil

TARTAR SAUCE
6 gherkins, minced
1 cup crème fraîche
2 tablespoons chopped parsley
2 tablespoons chopped dill
finely grated zest and juice
of 1 lemon

SERVES 4

PREPARATION + COOKING
20 + 16 minutes + chilling

STORAGE
Keep in the fridge for 2 days.

SERVE THIS WITH...
vegetable sticks
sweet potato wedges baked
in olive oil
(see page 65)
Apple & Pecan Tart
(see page 139)

1 Put the tuna, bread crumbs, ricotta, lemon zest, basil and egg in a bowl and mix well. Season with a little pepper.

2 Using floured hands, roll the mixture into 12 walnut-size balls. Dust lightly with flour.

3 Heat the olive oil in a frying pan over medium heat and fry the balls, in 2 batches, turning occasionally, until crisp, 6 to 8 minutes.

4 Meanwhile, make the tartar sauce by mixing all the ingredients together in a bowl. Serve with the fish balls.

cornmeal fish cakes

These crunchy fish cakes have a mild taste.

MAKES 8

PREPARATION + COOKING
15 + 30 minutes + chilling

STORAGE
Keep the fish cakes in the fridge
for 2 days and the dressing for
3 to 4 days.

SERVE THIS WITH...
Tartar Sauce (see page 107)
steamed vegetables
Summer Berry Ice Cups
   (see page 125)

HEALTH BENEFITS
White fish is a high-protein food
that is easily digestible. It is a
good source of selenium and
B vitamins, which can aid skin
health and support a healthy
immune system. White fish also
provides iodine—essential for
thyroid function and metabolism.
While white fish is lower in
essential omega-3 fats than oily
fish, it does contain some of
these beneficial fats, particularly
pollock and halibut.

7 ounces boiling potatoes,
   peeled and cut into chunks
4 ounces cod or pollock fillet
4 ounces smoked haddock fillet
   (finnan haddie)
1 shallot, minced
scant ⅔ cup milk

1 tablespoon chopped parsley
3 tablespoons rice flour
2 eggs, beaten
⅓ cup fine cornmeal
light olive oil, for frying
freshly ground black pepper

1 Cook the potatoes in a pan of boiling water until tender,
about 15 minutes.

2 Meanwhile, put the fish and shallot in a frying pan
and cover with the milk. Simmer until the fish is cooked
through, 3 to 4 minutes. Remove from the pan and let cool
slightly on a plate (discard the milk). Remove the skin and
flake the fish into a bowl with the shallot.

3 Drain the potatoes, return them to the pan and cook
for 1 minute to evaporate the excess moisture. Mash well.

4 Mix the flaked fish and shallots into the potatoes. Stir in
the parsley and season with black pepper.

5 With damp hands, shape the mixture into 8 small cakes.
Coat each cake in flour, dip in beaten egg and, finally, roll
in cornmeal. Refrigerate for 30 minutes to firm up.

6 Fry the fish cakes, in batches, until lightly brown, about
3 minutes per side. Drain on paper towels and serve.

creamy mackerel tarts

Your child will love these creamy little tarts.

1 recipe quantity Pastry
  (see page 43)
flour, for dusting
1 tablespoon light olive oil
1 leek, finely shredded
12 ounces smoked mackerel,
  skinned and chopped

3 eggs
heaped ¾ cup crème fraîche
finely grated zest of 1 lemon
½ cup grated Cheddar cheese
1 tablespoon minced dill

1 Preheat the oven to 350°F. Roll out the pastry on a floured surface and cut out 8 circles. Use to line 8 small tart pans.

2 Line the tart shells with parchment paper and fill with dried beans. Bake for 10 minutes, then remove the beans and paper and bake for 5 minutes longer to crisp the base. Remove from the oven.

3 Heat the oil in a frying pan, add the leek and fry for 3 to 4 minutes. Scatter the mackerel over the bottom of the tart shells, then add the leeks. Beat together the eggs, crème fraîche, lemon zest, Cheddar and dill. Pour the mixture into the pastry shells.

4 Bake until the filling is set and lightly golden on top, about 20 minutes. Remove from the oven and let cool for 15 minutes before serving.

MAKES 8

PREPARATION + COOKING
20 + 40 minutes

STORAGE
Keep in the fridge for 2 days.

SERVE THIS WITH...
steamed broccoli
mixed salad
Grilled Pineapple (see page 130)
plain yogurt

HEALTH BENEFITS
Mackerel is one of the best sources of omega-3 fatty acids to support your child's brain health and development. It is packed with nutrients, including vitamins B6 and B12, which are needed for red blood cell production, healthy nerve cells and the production of certain hormones and neurotransmitters. It is also one of the few good sources of vitamin D, which is essential for healthy bone formation.

shrimp & tomato fritters

These crunchy, bite-size fritters are made from shrimp and cherry tomatoes with a hint of ginger. Delicious hot or cold.

SERVES 4

PREPARATION + COOKING
15 + 15 minutes

STORAGE
Keep in the fridge for 1 day.

SERVE THIS WITH
Tomato Chutney (see page 105)
vegetable sticks
corn on the cob
Chunky Breadsticks (see page 87)
Almond-Chocolate Butter on
  Apple Wedges (see page 73)

HEALTH BENEFITS
Shellfish are packed with immune-boosting nutrients to support your child's health, including zinc, selenium and plenty of protein. Zinc is also important for growth and development during childhood, and activates areas of the brain that are involved with taste and smell. Low levels of zinc can be linked to poor appetite. Zinc is useful for treating childhood skin conditions, including eczema.

8 ounces peeled raw shrimp
½ cup all-purpose flour
8 cherry tomatoes, chopped
1 teaspoon baking powder
¾-inch piece fresh gingerroot, peeled and finely grated
1 tablespoon chopped cilantro
1 egg, beaten
pinch of cayenne pepper
2 tablespoons olive oil or coconut oil, for frying
sweet chili sauce, for serving

1 Put half the shrimp in a food processor with the flour, tomatoes, baking powder, ginger, cilantro, egg and cayenne. Pulse until minced.

2 Roughly chop the remaining shrimp and add to the mixture.

3 Heat half the olive oil in a frying pan. Drop about half of the mixture in 4 spoonfuls into the hot oil to make 4 fritters. Fry until golden brown, 2 to 3 minutes per side. Drain on paper towels. Repeat with the remaining mixture to make 4 more fritters.

4 Serve with the sweet chili sauce.

risotto cheese balls

These rice balls contain spinach and cheese.

3 tablespoons light olive oil
1 small onion, minced
2 garlic cloves, minced
heaped ½ cup risotto rice
2 cups hot low-sodium
   vegetable stock
6 sun-dried tomatoes in oil,
   drained and chopped

4 ounces baby leaf spinach
2 tablespoons grated Parmesan
   cheese
7 ounces mozzarella cheese,
   cut into 8 pieces
1 egg, beaten
heaped ¾ cup fine cornmeal

1 Heat 1 tablespoon of the oil in a saucepan and cook the onion over low heat until soft, about 5 minutes. Add the garlic and cook for 1 minute.
2 Stir in the rice, then gradually add the stock, one ladleful at a time, stirring constantly until absorbed.
3 Add the tomatoes, spinach and Parmesan and stir well. Season with black pepper and let cool for 1 hour.
4 Shape the mixture into 8 balls and push a piece of mozzarella into the center of each one. Flatten the balls slightly to form small cakes. Refrigerate for 30 minutes.
5 Put the beaten egg on one plate and the cornmeal on another. Dip the balls in the egg, then coat in cornmeal.
6 Heat the remaining olive oil in a frying pan and cook the cakes, in 2 batches, until golden brown, 4 to 5 minutes per side. Drain on paper towels and serve.

SERVES 4

PREPARATION + COOKING
20 + 40 minutes + cooling + chilling

STORAGE
Keep in the fridge for 1 day.

SERVE THIS WITH...
Chili-Tomato Sauce (see
   page 91)
steamed vegetables
Frozen Blueberry & Chocolate
   Slice (see page 135)

HEALTH BENEFITS
Mozzarella cheese is relatively low in fat and a rich source of protein and calcium. Just 1 ounce contains around 180mg calcium —over one-third of a young child's recommended daily intake. It also provides plenty of tryptophan, an amino acid that the body converts into serotonin, an important neurotransmitter for boosting mood.

078

vegetable samosas

Oven-baked samosas make a healthy meal.

SERVES 4

PREPARATION + COOKING
20 + 30 minutes

STORAGE
Keep in the fridge for 2 days.

SERVE THIS WITH
Raita (see page 58)
steamed green vegetables
Mango Ice Pops (see page 124)
Lemon-Coconut Macaroons
(see page 78)

HEALTH BENEFITS
A highly nutritious alternative
to ordinary potatoes, sweet
potatoes are packed with
antioxidants vitamin C and
beta-carotene. Beta-carotene,
which is converted by the body
to vitamin A, has antiviral and
skin-protecting properties. Sweet
potatoes are also a rich source
of vitamin E and, being high in
soluble fiber, can help to support
digestive health.

1 tablespoon light olive oil,
plus extra for greasing and
brushing
1 small red onion, chopped
1 garlic clove, minced
1 tablespoon medium curry
paste

1 carrot, peeled and finely diced
1 small sweet potato, peeled
and finely diced
scant ½ cup low-sodium
vegetable stock
scant ¼ cup frozen peas
4 phyllo sheets, each cut into 3

1 Heat the oil in a frying pan and sauté the onion until
soft, 2 to 3 minutes. Stir in the garlic and curry paste,
then add the carrot, sweet potato and vegetable stock.
Bring to a boil, then simmer until tender and all liquid has
evaporated. Stir in the peas and let cool.
2 Preheat the oven to 400°F. Grease 2 baking sheets.
3 Brush each strip of phyllo with oil. Put a spoonful of
vegetables on each strip and fold over into a triangle.
Keep folding over to the end of the strip. Brush with oil.
4 Bake 6 triangles per sheet until crisp, about 20 minutes.

sweet potato falafels

These energizing bites are gluten-free.

SERVES 4

PREPARATION + COOKING
20 minutes + 1 hour + chilling

STORAGE
Keep in the fridge for 2 days.

SERVE THIS WITH...
warm wholewheat pita breads
mixed salad
Fruit Slice (see page 136)

1 sweet potato
5 ounces firm tofu, drained
1 jarred, roasted red bell
    pepper in oil, drained and
    chopped
1 teaspoon ground cumin
1 garlic clove, minced
1 teaspoon ground coriander
1 tablespoon chopped cilantro
1 tablespoon lemon juice
heaped ½ cup chickpea flour

¾ cup sesame seeds
light olive oil, for greasing
freshly ground black pepper

TAHINI-YOGURT DRESSING
1 tablespoon tahini
2 tablespoons plain yogurt
1 tablespoon lemon juice
1 teaspoon raw cane sugar
    or xylitol

1 Preheat the oven to 425°F.

2 Roast the sweet potato until tender, about 45 minutes. Let cool, then peel. Turn the oven down to 400°F.

3 Put all the ingredients, except the sesame seeds, in a large bowl and mash with a potato masher. Season with black pepper. If the mixture is wet, add a little more flour. Refrigerate for 30 minutes to firm up.

4 Put the seeds on a plate. Mold the mixture into 12 balls, then roll in the seeds. Put on a greased, parchment-lined baking sheet. Bake until crisp, about 15 minutes.

5 Mix the dressing ingredients together and refrigerate until needed. Serve the falafels hot or cold with the dressing.

HEALTH BENEFITS
Chickpea flour, also known as gram flour, is simply dried chickpeas ground to a flour-like consistency. It is wheat- and gluten-free and easy to digest. High in fiber and protein, it is perfect for balancing blood sugar. It is also a rich source of vitamin A, vitamin K for bone health and several B vitamins including thiamine, riboflavin, niacin, pantothenic acid and folate. A good vegetarian source of iron, too, with 1 cup supplying 4.5mg—over half the daily requirement for children.

*crisp tofu skewers

HEALTH BENEFITS
Tofu is an excellent source of protein, providing all the essential amino acids for growth and development. It is also a useful source of omega-3 fatty acids for vegetarians and contains plenty of B vitamins, calcium and iron.

These chunks of tofu are coated in a sweet tomato-soy marinade and covered with sesame seeds to create a crisp finish. This is an energizing protein-packed meal with nutrients to support your child's growth.

2 tablespoons tamari soy sauce
1 tablespoon honey or agave
 nectar
1 tablespoon light olive oil,
 plus extra for greasing
1 tablespoon tomato paste

½ teaspoon wholegrain
 mustard
pinch of cayenne pepper
1 pound firm tofu, drained and
 cut into ¾-inch cubes
heaped ⅓ cup sesame seeds

SERVES 4

PREPARATION + COOKING
15 + 10 minutes + marinating

STORAGE
Keep in the fridge for 2 days.

SERVE THIS WITH...
Tomato Chutney (see page 105)
mixed salad leaves
cucumber sticks
baby corn

1 To make the marinade, mix together the soy sauce, honey, oil, tomato paste, mustard and cayenne pepper. Put the tofu in a shallow dish and pour the marinade over. Stir to coat thoroughly. Let marinate in the fridge for at least 1 hour or overnight.

2 Soak 8 wooden skewers in water for 30 minutes. Preheat the broiler. Lightly grease a baking sheet and line it with parchment paper.

3 Put the sesame seeds on a plate. Thread the tofu onto the soaked skewers, then roll in the sesame seeds to coat.

4 Lay the skewers on the prepared baking sheet and broil, 4 to 5 inches from the heat, until golden and crisp, about 5 minutes per side. Remove the skewers before serving.

SERVES 4

lima-bean burgers

PREPARATION + COOKING
15 + 40 minutes

STORAGE
Keep in the fridge for 2 days or freeze for up to 1 month.

SERVE THIS WITH...
small wholewheat buns
mixed salad
sliced tomato
Frozen Pineapple Cheesecake
Slice (see page 138)

HEALTH BENEFITS
Red onions are particularly high in quercetin—a powerful antioxidant that can help reduce inflammation and lower histamine, making it beneficial for tackling allergies. Red onion is also a good source of chromium—a mineral needed to metabolize carbohydrates and balance blood sugar levels.

These creamy burgers contain a touch of pesto, which gives them a special summery Mediterranean flavor. Lima beans are soft textured and mild in flavor, making them an ideal vegetarian protein food for babies and young children. Easy to make, these burgers can also be baked in the oven from frozen. Serve in little buns for a healthy fun meal.

light olive oil, for greasing
28 ounces canned lima beans, drained and rinsed
3 tablespoons red pesto
1 egg, beaten

heaped 2 cups soft wholewheat bread crumbs
1 red onion, grated
freshly ground black pepper

1 Preheat the oven to 425°F. Lightly grease a baking sheet and line it with parchment paper.
2 Put the beans and pesto in a food processor and pulse until smooth. Add the egg, bread crumbs and onion and pulse to mix. Season with black pepper.
3 With damp hands, shape the mixture into 8 little burgers. Put on the prepared baking sheet and bake until golden and crisp, 30 to 40 minutes. Serve hot.

almond pizza

This is a delicious alternative to regular pizza.

1 cup tomato purée
6 cherry tomatoes, halved
½ red onion, thinly sliced
3 jarred, roasted red bell
   peppers in oil, drained and
   chopped
¼ cup pitted sliced black olives
7 ounces buffalo mozzarella
   cheese, torn into pieces
½ cup grated Cheddar cheese

BASE
heaped 2 cups soft wholewheat
   bread crumbs
2 garlic cloves, minced
1 cup ground almonds
heaped 1 cup sliced almonds
1 stick unsalted butter, melted
2 eggs, beaten

1 Preheat the oven to 350°F. Lightly grease a 13- x 9-inch jelly roll pan and line it with parchment paper.
2 To make the base, put all the ingredients in a large bowl and mix well, then press into the pan to form a thin crust.
3 Bake until just lightly colored, about 10 minutes.
4 Spread the tomato purée over the base, then top with the remaining ingredients.
5 Bake until the cheese is bubbling, 10 to 15 minutes. Let cool slightly, then cut into slices to serve.

SERVES 8

PREPARATION + COOKING
20 + 25 minutes

STORAGE
Keep in the fridge for 2 days.

SERVE THIS WITH...
mixed salad
vegetable sticks
Peaches with Berry Syrup
   (see page 128)

HEALTH BENEFITS
The Mediterranean vegetables—bell peppers, tomatoes, red onion, olives and garlic—used in this dish are well known for their anti-inflammatory and antioxidant properties, which can help with common conditions such as asthma and skin complaints, including eczema.

tapas soufflé omelet

This chunky, fluffy omelet can be cut into wedges, making it ideal finger food.

SERVES 4

PREPARATION + COOKING
10 + 5 minutes

STORAGE
Keep in the fridge for 1 day.

SERVE THIS WITH…
mixed salad
Squash Scones (see page 82)
fresh fruit
plain yogurt

HEALTH BENEFITS
Globe artichokes have detoxifying qualities and help the liver function more efficiently. This is particularly useful if your child suffers with any allergies, poor skin or inflammation. Compounds in the artichoke increase the production of bile, which aids digestion, so may help to alleviate irritable bowel or stomach troubles.

6 eggs, separated
¼ cup crumbled feta cheese
4 marinated artichoke hearts in oil, drained and chopped
1 jarred, roasted red pepper in oil, drained and chopped
2 tablespoons sliced marinated mushrooms
1 tablespoon chopped chives
1 tablespoon olive oil or coconut oil, for frying
freshly ground black pepper

1 Put the egg yolks in a bowl and beat well. Stir in the feta and vegetables. Season with a little black pepper.

2 Put the egg whites in a separate bowl and beat until stiff peaks form. Carefully fold the egg yolk mixture into the egg whites. Sprinkle in the chives.

3 Preheat the broiler. Heat the oil in a frying pan. Pour in the egg mixture and cook for 1 to 2 minutes. Put the pan under the broiler, close to the heat, and cook until golden brown, about 2 minutes. Remove from the pan and cut into wedges to serve.

mini vegetable quiches

These quiches are delicious hot or cold.

1 recipe quantity Pastry
  (see page 43)
11 ounces broccolini, cut into
  ¾-inch pieces
1 garlic clove, minced
1 tablespoon light olive oil

1 cup crème fraîche
4 eggs
8 sun-dried tomatoes in oil,
  drained and minced
freshly ground black pepper

MAKES 4

PREPARATION + COOKING
20 + 45 minutes + chilling
+ freezing

STORAGE
Keep in the fridge for 2 days
or freeze for up to 1 month.

SERVE THIS WITH...
mixed salad
vegetable sticks
Ice-Cream Sandwiches
  (see page 126)

HEALTH BENEFITS
When you use 100% wholewheat
products, the wheat bran and
germ remain. These are packed
with health-promoting nutrients,
including selenium, magnesium,
B vitamins and manganese. You
also increase the fiber intake and
slow the rate at which sugars
are broken down and released
into the bloodstream. This
helps to keep you feeling fuller
for longer and helps to prevent
mid-morning and mid-afternoon
energy slumps.

1 Roll out the pastry on a floured surface and cut out
4 rounds. Use to line 4 tartlet pans that are 3 inches in
diameter. Refrigerate for 15 minutes. Meanwhile, preheat
the oven to 375°F.
2 Line the tart shells with parchment paper and fill with
dried beans. Bake for 10 minutes. Remove the beans
and paper and bake for 5 minutes longer. Remove from
the oven. Reduce the temperature to 350°F.
3 To make the filling, blanch the broccolini in boiling
water for 1 minute, then drain and dry with a dish towel.
4 Sauté the garlic in the oil for 1 minute, then add the
broccolini and stir for 1 minute. Season with pepper.
5 Beat together the crème fraîche and eggs until smooth,
then add the broccolini and garlic. Stir in the tomatoes.
6 Spoon the filling into the pastry shells and bake until set
and golden on top, 20 to 25 minutes.

085

Ⓥ Ⓞ Ⓧ Ⓓ Ⓑ Ⓕ Ⓦ

mixed pepper tartlets

MAKES 8

These make wonderful party and picnic food.

PREPARATION + COOKING
20 + 20 minutes

STORAGE
Keep in the fridge for 2 days.

SERVE THIS WITH...
sweet potato wedges baked in
  olive oil
baby corn
snow peas
Coconut Squares
  (see page 127)

HEALTH BENEFITS
Red bell peppers contain high
levels of the antioxidants vitamin
C, beta-carotene, vitamin E and
zinc to help support immune
health. Vitamin C and the
magnesium in peppers are
important for tackling stress and
boosting energy production. The
carotenoids present, such as
lutein and zeaxanthin, are also
vital for healthy eyesight.

1 tablespoon light olive oil,
  plus extra for greasing
  and brushing
8 phyllo pastry sheets
2 bell peppers (1 yellow and
  1 red), halved and seeded

1 tomato, diced
1 teaspoon balsamic vinegar
scant ¾ cup ricotta cheese
2 tablespoons chopped basil
1 garlic clove, minced
freshly ground black pepper

1 Preheat the oven to 350°F. Lightly grease 8 cups
in a muffin pan.
2 Cut a sheet of phyllo into 4 squares and brush with
a little oil. Stack the 4 squares on top of each other at
different angles. Push the stack into a muffin cup and
brush again with oil. Repeat with the remaining phyllo.
3 Bake until golden, 8 to 10 minutes. Let cool in the pan
for 5 minutes, then transfer to a wire rack to cool.
4 Heat the broiler, then broil the pepper halves, cut-side
down, on a baking sheet until blackened, about 8 minutes.
Let cool for 5 minutes, then peel away the skin and dice the
flesh. Put in a bowl with the tomato, oil and vinegar and
season with black pepper. Mix well.
5 Blitz the ricotta, basil and garlic in a food processor
until combined. Put a spoonful in each phyllo shell and
top with the mixed pepper mixture.

carrot & cheese roulade

This is a light but protein-rich dish.

1 tablespoon olive oil, plus
   extra for greasing
1½ cups grated carrot
1½ cups grated zucchini
4 eggs, separated

1 tablespoon chopped parsley
heaped ¼ cup grated Parmesan
   cheese
1 cup herbed cream cheese
freshly ground black pepper

1 Preheat the oven to 400°F. Lightly grease a 12- x
10-inch jelly roll pan and line with parchment paper.
2 Sauté the carrots and zucchini in the oil until soft, 2
to 3 minutes. Spoon into a colander to drain and let cool.
3 Transfer to a bowl and beat in the egg yolks and parsley.
Season to taste with black pepper.
4 Put the egg whites in a separate bowl and beat until
stiff peaks form. Stir a spoonful into the carrot mixture to
loosen it, then carefully fold in the rest.
5 Gently spoon the mixture into the prepared pan. Bake
until light golden brown and firm, 12 to 15 minutes.
6 Put a large sheet of parchment paper on the worktop
and sprinkle with the Parmesan cheese. Carefully unmold
the vegetable cake onto the paper and cover the top with
a clean dish towel. Let cool.
7 Gently spread the cream cheese over the cake, leaving a
³⁄₈-inch border. Roll up from a short side. Slice to serve.

SERVES 8

PREPARATION + COOKING
15 + 20 minutes

STORAGE
Keep in the fridge for 2 days.

SERVE THIS WITH...
vegetable sticks
Chunky Breadsticks (see page 87)
Mango-Orange Crêpes
  (see page 131)

HEALTH BENEFITS
Beta-carotene-rich foods such
as carrots are excellent for
children's immune and skin
health. Beta-carotene is a
precursor to vitamin A, which
is strongly antiviral. Carrots are
important for the production of
T cells in the digestive tract,
which help the immune system
to respond appropriately to
beneficial bacteria and harmful
microbes and protect mucosal
surfaces against infection.

DESSERTS

The recipes in this chapter show you how easy it is to create delicious desserts that are healthy and nourishing. All the dishes included are based on fruit, whole grains, nuts and seeds, and are either naturally sugar-free or use just a small amount of sugar. They include plenty of protein to help keep blood sugar levels balanced, avoiding the sugar highs and lows often associated with children's sweet treats. There are many delicious options to choose from, such as cooling Mango Ice Pops and Ice-Cream Sandwiches, as well as Sweet Cherry Samosas and Banana Choc-Nut Bites. The whole family will adore these scrumptious dishes—desserts will never be the same again!

087

mango ice pops

MAKES 4–6

PREPARATION
10 minutes + freezing

STORAGE
Freeze for 1 month.

SERVE THIS WITH...
Tostada Chili Wedges
(see page 53)

HEALTH BENEFITS
Mangoes are packed with antioxidants, including vitamins C and E and beta-carotene, which is important for protecting the body against harmful free radicals and supporting immune function. Rich in soluble fiber and water, mangoes can improve digestive health and ease constipation. Beta-carotene helps to neutralize the harmful effects of UV light—useful for protecting the skin during the summer heat.

Ripe mangoes are naturally sweet and bursting with nutrients to keep your baby or child healthy and fighting fit. This simple fruit-filled ice pop is an easy way to boost their intake of fruit as well as keeping them hydrated on a hot day. Unlike commercial ice pops, there are no sugars or sweeteners added—just pure fruit!

2 oranges
1 large, ripe mango, pitted and
    cut into chunks

1 Juice the oranges and pour the juice into a blender. Add the mango and blend until smooth.
2 Pour the mixture into 4 or 6 ice popsicle molds, depending on size. Freeze until the ice pops are set, 3 to 4 hours or overnight.

summer berry ice cups

Scoops of this sensational dairy-free ice "cream" are served in little nut cases.

2 bananas, chopped
⅔ cup cashew nuts
scant 1 cup pomegranate juice
2 cups frozen mixed summer
    berries

NUT CUPS
1 heaped cup cashew nuts
scant ½ cup dried shredded
    coconut
⅓ cup pitted dates
2 tablespoons orange juice
light olive oil, for greasing

1 Freeze the bananas for 4 hours or overnight.

2 To make the nut cups, put the cashew nuts and coconut into a blender and blend until fine. Tip into a bowl.

3 Put the dates and orange juice into the blender and blend to a purée, adding water, if needed, to form a stiff paste.

4 Mix the date paste into the dry ingredients with your hands to form a crumbly dough.

5 Line 4 tartlet pans or 4 cups in a muffin pan with plastic wrap. Lightly oil the wrap. Press in the dough to shape cups. Freeze for 1 hour to firm up. Remove from the pans.

6 Put the cashew nuts and pomegranate juice in a blender and process until creamy. Add the frozen berries and bananas and pulse to form a soft, smooth ice "cream." Put a spoonful of ice "cream" in each nut cup and serve.

SERVES 4

PREPARATION
15 minutes + freezing

STORAGE
Keep the ice "cream" in the freezer for 1 month. Keep the nut cups in the fridge for 1 week or freeze for 1 month. Note that the recipe makes more ice cream than you will need for the cups.

SERVE THIS WITH...
Italian Tuna Balls (see page 106)

HEALTH BENEFITS
100% pure pomegranate juice is an easy way to boost your child's intake of powerful antioxidant compounds, including polyphenols and bioflavonoids, which, together with their high vitamin C content, help to support the body's immune system and protect brain cells from damage. These nutrients can also help to strengthen collagen, which is an essential component for healthy skin and bones.

ice-cream sandwiches

Choc-mint ice cream served in chocolate wafers. The coconut milk makes the ice cream dairy free.

MAKES 6

PREPARATION + COOKING
30 + 5 minutes + freezing + setting + softening

STORAGE
Freeze for up to 1 month.

SERVE THIS WITH…
Spicy Chicken Kebabs (see page 94)

HEALTH BENEFITS
Green superfood powders, such as chlorella, spirulina, wheatgrass and barley grass, are all packed with chlorophyll, amino acids and a whole range of vitamins and minerals to nourish children and keep them energized. They are a great addition to a child's diet, especially if you are concerned about them eating sufficient greens, or if they are feeling low in energy or have a poor appetite.

2 drops of peppermint extract
1 teaspoon green superfood powder
¾ cup cashew nuts
3 mint leaves
scant 1 cup canned coconut milk
2 tablespoons raw cane sugar or xylitol
3 tablespoons semi-sweet chocolate chips or cacao nibs

WAFERS
5½ ounces semi-sweet chocolate, chopped
2 tablespoons raw cane sugar or xylitol
1 tablespoon olive oil or coconut oil
scant ½ cup chopped toasted nuts

1 Put all the ingredients for the ice cream, except the chocolate chips, in a blender and blend until completely smooth. Stir in the chocolate chips. Pour into 6 small ramekins and freeze until firm, about 4 hours.

2 To make the wafers, melt the chocolate in a pan with the sugar and olive oil, then stir in the nuts. Use a spoon to form 12 circles of the mixture on a sheet of parchment paper—the circles should be as big as the ramekins. Let set, about 2 hours.

3 Remove the ice cream from the ramekins, set each one on a wafer and top with a second wafer. Let soften for 15 minutes before eating.

coconut squares

Squares of fruit gelatin on an oaty coconut base.

2 passion fruit, halved
1 ripe mango, pitted and diced
½ to 1 cup apple cider
2 tablespoons olive oil or
   coconut oil
4 tablespoons vegetarian
   gelatin or agar agar flakes

BASE
light olive oil, for greasing
heaped 1 cup dried shredded
   coconut
1¼ cups rolled oats
heaped ⅔ cup pitted dates
2 tablespoons orange juice

1 Lightly grease and line a shallow 8-inch square pan.

2 To make the base, put the coconut and oats in a food processor and pulse to break down slightly. Add the dates and orange juice and blitz to bring the mixture together.

3 Press into the prepared pan and freeze for 30 minutes.

4 Rub the passion fruit pulp through a strainer; discard the seeds. Put the pulp and juice in a blender with the mango and blend until smooth. Add enough apple cider to make 2 cups.

5 Pour into a pan and add the olive oil. Sprinkle the gelatin over the liquid. Simmer for 5 minutes, stirring to dissolve. Remove from the heat and let cool slightly.

6 Pour the gelatin mixture over the coconut base and refrigerate until set, 3 to 4 hours or overnight. Cut into squares to serve.

MAKES 12–16

PREPARATION + COOKING
20 + 5 minutes + freezing + chilling

STORAGE
Keep in the fridge for 3 to 4 days.

SERVE THIS WITH...
Tandoori Chicken Strips
  (see page 44)
naan bread

HEALTH BENEFITS
A great energy-booster, passion fruit is packed with B vitamins, iron, magnesium, vitamin C and fiber, which are all needed to maintain energy levels, support the nervous system and keep the brain and body fueled, especially during times of stress. It is also a good source of vitamin A, which is important for maintaining healthy mucus membranes and skin.

HEALTH BENEFITS
Peaches and nectarines provide good amounts of antioxidants, including carotenoids such as lycopene and lutein. These can help to protect against disease, support immune health and maintain healthy eyes and skin. Peaches also provide a useful source of potassium, which can help to maintain proper fluid balance and help regulate nerve and muscle activity.

peaches with berry syrup

This simple, summery dessert is delicious warm or cold. Cutting the peaches into wedges makes them a perfect finger food, and they are delicious dipped into the sweet strawberry syrup. You could also thread the wedges onto skewers and broil them lightly.

4 ripe peaches, halved, pitted
and thickly sliced
3 tablespoons raw cane sugar
or xylitol

1½ cups strawberries
1 tablespoon arrowroot or
cornstarch

SERVES 4

PREPARATION + COOKING
15 + 7 minutes

STORAGE
Keep in the fridge for 1 day.

SERVE THIS WITH...
Beet & Beef Mini Burgers
(see page 102)
mixed salad
wholewheat rolls

1 Preheat the broiler. Put some foil over the rack in the broiler pan.

2 Spread the peach slices on the foil and sprinkle with 2 tablespoons of the sugar.

3 Broil, 3 to 4 inches from the heat, until the wedges are golden brown, 4 to 5 minutes.

4 Meanwhile, make the strawberry syrup: Put the strawberries, arrowroot and remaining sugar in a blender and blend until smooth. Pour into a small pan and heat gently, stirring all the time, until the sauce thickens slightly, 1 to 2 minutes. Pour into a little bowl for dipping, and serve with the peach slices.

092

Ⓥ Ⓟ Ⓧ Ⓧ Ⓞ ⊜ ◉

grilled pineapple

Pineapple skewers with orange-coconut cream.

2 teaspoons arrowroot or
  cornstarch
finely grated zest and juice of
  2 oranges
2 tablespoons raw cane sugar
  or xylitol

1 small, ripe pineapple,
  quartered, peeled, cored
  and sliced into thick wedges
light olive oil, for greasing
8 ounces silken tofu
½ cup dried shredded coconut

1 Soak 8 wooden skewers in water for 30 minutes.

2 Meanwhile, put the arrowroot in a small pan with a
little of the orange juice and mix to form a smooth paste.
Gradually mix in the remaining juice, then add the sugar
and zest. Stir over low heat until the sugar dissolves and
the sauce thickens slightly, 2 to 3 minutes. Let cool.

3 Put 16 of the pineapple wedges in a shallow dish and
pour the orange sauce over. Turn to coat. Thread 2 wedges
onto each skewer.

4 Heat a ridged grill pan, then lightly grease it with oil.
Pan-grill the pineapple skewers, in batches, until golden
brown, 1 to 2 minutes per side.

5 Put the tofu, coconut and remaining pineapple in a
blender and blend until smooth. Pour into a bowl to serve
with the pineapple (remove the skewers before serving).

mango-orange crêpes

These fruity wholegrain crêpes are packed full of vitamins, and delicious too!

½ cup all-purpose white flour
½ cup wholewheat flour
1 tablespoon ground flaxseed
finely grated zest of 2 oranges
3 eggs
generous 1⅓ cups milk
2 tablespoons olive oil or
    coconut oil

FILLING
2 mangoes, pitted and chopped
1 tablespoon lemon juice
1 tablespoon raw cane sugar
    or xylitol

1 To make the crêpes, put the flours, flaxseed, orange zest, eggs and milk into a blender and blend until smooth.
2 Heat half of the olive oil in a small crêpe or frying pan. Pour in a little batter and swirl it around. Cook over high heat until the top is dry, 1 to 2 minutes, then flip over and cook the underside briefly, about 1 minute. Remove from the pan. Repeat with the remaining batter, adding the remaining oil to the pan if needed. The batter should make 8 crêpes; stack them, interleaved with parchment paper.
3 To make the mango filling, put all the ingredients in a blender and blend to form a thick purée.
4 Spread a little of the mango purée over each crêpe and roll up tightly. Slice across into rounds and serve.

MAKES 8

PREPARATION + COOKING
15 + 25 minutes

STORAGE
Keep in the fridge for 2 days or freeze for up to 1 month.

SERVE THIS WITH...
Crisp Spiced Shrimp
    (see page 58)

HEALTH BENEFITS
Flaxseed, also known as linseed, is one of the richest plant sources of omega-3 fatty acids—important for brain function, cell health and combating inflammation in the body. Flaxseed is also high in soluble fiber, making it a useful remedy for easing constipation.

094

sweet cherry samosas

These triangles are served with mint sugar.

MAKES 6

PREPARATION + COOKING
20 + 15 minutes

STORAGE
Keep in the fridge for 3 days.

SERVE THIS WITH...
Tandoori Chicken Strips
(see page 44)

HEALTH BENEFITS
Peppermint is a well-known
digestive aid and is particularly
useful for relieving flatulence and
indigestion and easing muscle
spasms. Suitable for even young
children, cooled peppermint tea
is a useful remedy for irritable
bowel and stomach upsets.

9 ouncess sweet cherries,
    pitted and chopped
2 tablespoons pure fruit
    cherry jam
5 tablespoons butter, melted
12 phyllo pastry strips, each
    cut to 2½ x 10 inches
raw cane sugar, for sprinkling

MINT-SUGAR DIP
8 mint leaves
¼ cup raw cane sugar or xylitol
1 tablespoon vitamin C powder
½ teaspoon baking soda

1 Make the filling by mixing the cherries and jam in a bowl.
2 Preheat the oven to 400°F. Lightly grease a baking sheet
with a little butter. Line the sheet with parchment paper.
3 Spread out a strip of phyllo and brush with some melted
butter. Lay another strip on top and butter it.
4 Put a small amount of cherry filling on one end of the
strip and fold one corner of the pastry over the filling to
form a triangle. Continue folding the pastry over to the
end of the strip to make a triangular samosa. Repeat with
the remaining phyllo and filling to make 6 samosas.
5 Spread them on the baking sheet, brush with butter and
sprinkle with sugar. Bake until golden, 10 to 15 minutes.
6 Put all the dip ingredients in a blender and blend until
smooth. Put in a small bowl. Serve with the samosas.

lemon cheesecake

Creamy and utterly delicious.

light olive oil, for greasing
¾ heaped cup cashew nuts
1 cup rolled oats
finely grated zest of 1 lemon
juice of ½ lemon
⅓ cup melted coconut oil
2 tablespoons raw cane sugar
    or xylitol

TOPPING
scant 1 cup Greek yogurt
1½ cups cream cheese
2 eggs
finely grated zest and juice of
    2 lemons
2 tablespoons all-purpose flour
3 tablespoons raw cane sugar
    or xylitol

MAKES 15 SLICES

PREPARATION + COOKING
20 + 50 minutes + chilling
+ cooling

STORAGE
Keep in the fridge for 3 days.

SERVE THIS WITH...
Herby Koftas (see page 99)
wholewheat pitas

HEALTH BENEFITS
Greek yogurt has a mild, creamy taste that young children adore, but opt for plain yogurt only as most fruit yogurts are laden with sugar and sweeteners. Look for authentic Greek yogurt rather than "Greek style," which often contains thickeners or stabilizers to create a thicker texture and increase shelf life. When choosing a brand, the fewer ingredients in the yogurt the better. Look for plain yogurt that contains just milk or milk and cream and live active yogurt culture.

1 Preheat the oven to 400°F. Grease an 8-inch square shallow pan and line it with parchment paper.
2 Put the cashew nuts in a food processor and blitz to grind finely. Add the oats and pulse lightly. Tip into a large bowl and mix with the lemon zest and juice.
3 Heat the oil in a small pan with the sugar until warm, then pour over the oat mixture and stir to combine. Spoon into the prepared pan and press down firmly.
4 Bake until lightly firm, about 10 minutes. Let cool for 5 minutes. Reduce the heat to 350°F.
5 Put the topping ingredients in a food processor and blitz until smooth. Pour over the base and bake until the topping is set and lightly colored, 35 to 40 minutes. Turn off the oven and let cool inside, then chill.

banana choc-nut bites

Choc-nut bananas in crisp phyllo pastry.

SERVES 4

PREPARATION + COOKING
15 + 10 minutes

STORAGE
Keep in the fridge for 1 day.

SERVE THIS WITH...
Italian Tuna Balls (see page 106)

HEALTH BENEFITS
Bananas are a well-known energizing fruit, containing natural sugars and B vitamins, which the body needs to produce energy. Vitamins B5 and B6 also help support the nervous system and combat the effects of stress. Bananas are a great mood-booster, too, being a natural source of the amino acid tryptophan, which the body converts into the "feel good" neurotransmitter serotonin.

light olive oil, for greasing
2 tablespoons cashew nut
   butter
2 ounces semi-sweet
   chocolate, grated

8 sheets of phyllo pastry
2 tablespoons butter, melted
2 bananas, chopped

1 Preheat the oven to 400°F. Lightly grease 2 baking sheets and line with parchment paper.

2 Mix together the cashew nut butter and chocolate.

3 Lay 2 sheets of phyllo on the worktop, one on top of the other. Brush the top with melted butter.

4 Put one-fourth of the banana lengthwise in the center of the pastry, leaving a ¾-inch gap at the sides. Top with one-fourth of the chocolate mixture.

5 Fold in both sides of the pastry, then roll up to enclose the filling. Put seam-side down on one of the baking sheets. Repeat with the remaining phyllo sheets to make 4 parcels. Brush with butter and bake for 10 minutes.

frozen blueberry & chocolate slice

A great celebration dessert for parties.

3 tablespoons melted
   coconut oil
¾ heaped cup cashew nuts
1 cup blueberries, fresh or
   frozen
finely grated zest of 1 lemon
1 tablespoon lemon juice
generous 1 cup grape juice or
   other berry juice
1 tablespoon unsweetened
   cocoa powder (optional)

BASE
light olive oil, for greasing
1 cup almonds
1 tablespoon ground flaxseed
1 teaspoon ground cinnamon
pinch of salt
1 tablespoon unsweetened
   cocoa powder
scant ⅔ cup raisins
1 teaspoon vanilla extract
⅓ cup melted coconut oil

1 Lightly grease an 8-inch square cake pan with oil and line it with parchment paper.

2 For the base, put the almonds, flaxseed, cinnamon, salt and cocoa powder in a food processor and blitz to form small crumbs. Add the raisins, vanilla extract and oil. Pulse until the mixture forms a dough. Press into the pan and refrigerate while you make the filling.

3 Put the remaining ingredients in a blender and blend until smooth. Pour evenly over the base. Freeze for 4 hours before cutting into slices.

MAKES 12 SLICES

PREPARATION + COOKING
20 minutes + 4 minutes
+ freezing

STORAGE
Freeze for up to 1 month.

SERVE THIS WITH...
Crisp Drumsticks (see page 92)

HEALTH BENEFITS
Blueberries are a wonderful superfood for your child's brain, bursting with powerful protective and immune-supporting antioxidants, including anthocyanidins, vitamins C and E, selenium and zinc. Zinc is an essential mineral to help the brain turn glucose into energy as well as being needed for the production of hormones and neurotransmitters for brain function.

*fruit slice

HEALTH BENEFITS
Raspberries are bursting with vitamins and antioxidants to help protect the body's cells and tissues against damage. They are a good source of B vitamins, including folate and niacin, which are important for the production of neurotransmitters to aid brain function. They also contain lots of soluble fiber, which, together with the protein from the nuts, will help to keep blood sugar levels even through the day.

This delicious moist tart can be enjoyed hot or cold and has a low glycemic index to help keep blood sugar levels even throughout the day. It contains no wheat or gluten and is packed with protein, calcium, magnesium and fiber. The eggs provide memory-boosting nutrients.

light olive oil, for greasing
2 ripe pears, cored and diced
3 eggs, separated
¼ cup raw cane sugar or xylitol
2½ cups ground almonds

1 teaspoon ground cinnamon
1 teaspoon gluten-free baking
   powder
1⅔ cups frozen raspberries

MAKES 12

PREPARATION + COOKING
20 + 40 minutes

STORAGE
Keep in the fridge for 3 days or
freeze for up to 1 month.

SERVE THIS WITH...
Tapas Soufflé Omelet
  (see page 118)
mixed salad

1 Preheat the oven to 350°F. Lightly grease a shallow
8- x 12-inch pan with oil and line it with parchment paper.
2 Put the pears, egg yolks and sugar in a food processor
and blitz until thick and creamy. Add the ground almonds,
cinnamon and baking powder and blitz until combined.
3 Put the egg whites in a bowl and beat until stiff peaks
form. Carefully fold the egg whites into the pear mixture,
then add the raspberries.
4 Pour the batter into the prepared pan. Bake until golden
and firm to touch, 30 to 40 minutes. Let cool in the pan
before cutting into slices.

frozen pineapple cheesecake slice

A delicious tropical-flavored frozen bar.

SERVES 10–12

PREPARATION
20 minutes + freezing

STORAGE
Keep in the fridge for 3 days or freeze for up to 1 month.

SERVE THIS WITH...
Risotto Cheese Balls (see page 111)
mixed salad

HEALTH BENEFITS
Pineapple is rich in the protein-digesting enzyme bromelain, which promotes healthy digestion and may help to ease constipation. As it is able to break down areas of inflamed body tissue, pineapple can help reduce inflammation and swelling, making it useful for alleviating symptoms associated with conditions such as asthma. Eating pineapple between meals maximizes bromelain's anti-inflammatory effect.

light olive oil, for greasing
1 cup walnut pieces
heaped ⅓ cup cashew nuts
¼ cup melted coconut oil
3 tablespoons ground flaxseed
finely grated zest of 1 lime
⅓ cup chopped pitted dates
1 tablespoon raw cane sugar or xylitol

TOPPING
generous 1 cup canned coconut milk
½ heaped cup cashew nuts
2 cups fresh pineapple chunks
2 tablespoons raw cane sugar or xylitol
finely grated zest of 1 lime
1 tablespoon lime juice

1 Lightly grease an 8-inch square shallow pan and line it with parchment paper.
2 To make the base, put the walnuts and cashew nuts in a food processor and pulse to form fine crumbs. Add the remaining ingredients and blitz to form a crumbly mix.
3 Press the mixture into the prepared pan and chill.
4 To make the topping, put all the ingredients into a blender and blend until thick and creamy. Pour over the base and freeze for at least 3 hours.
5 Remove from the freezer 30 minutes before serving.

apple & pecan tarts

These tarts have a spiced apple and raisin filling.

2 cups chopped pecans
1 cup rolled oats
1 teaspoon ground cinnamon
⅓ cup chopped pitted dates
juice of 1 orange

FILLING
2 apples, peeled, cored and
  roughly chopped
1 teaspoon ground cinnamon
2 tablespoons raw cane sugar
  or xylitol
1 handful of raisins

1 To make the tart shells, put the pecans in a food processor and blitz until finely ground. Add the oats and pulse to break up slightly. Tip into a bowl and stir in the cinnamon.

2 Put the dates and orange juice in a blender and blend to form a paste. Add to the oat mixture and mix with your hands to form a crumbly dough. Press the dough into six tartlet pans or cups in a muffin pan to make tart shells.

3 To make the filling, put the apples, cinnamon and sugar in a pan with a splash of water and gently cook until soft, about 4 minutes. Mash with a potato masher to form a chunky pureé. Remove from the heat and stir in the raisins. Let cool, then spoon into the tart shells. Remove the tarts from the pans and serve.

MAKES 6

PREPARATION + COOKING
20 + 5 minutes

STORAGE
Keep in the fridge for 2 to
3 days.

SERVE THIS WITH...
Crisp Pork Bites (see page 97)

HEALTH BENEFITS
Dates are naturally sweet and energizing, but thanks to their fiber content they can also help to moderate the speed at which they release their sugars into the bloodstream. They are a perfect pick-me-up after exercise, especially when combined with some protein such as a handful of nuts. A good source of iron and magnesium, they can be useful when children are feeling fatigued.

menu plans

wheat- & gluten-free 5-day menu

Many of the recipes in this book are suitable for those on a wheat- or gluten-free diet or who are wishing to reduce their intake of wheat and gluten, which can be common allergies in children. If your child is a celiac, a lifelong exclusion of all gluten grains (wheat, barley, rye and contaminated oats) is essential. However, you will find many delicious, safe options for your child to enjoy in this book.

Day 1

Breakfast: Raisin-Quinoa Slices (see page 28) and fresh fruit

Lunch: Crisp Spiced Shrimp (see page 58) and crudités; fresh fruit and yogurt

Dinner: Thai-Spiced Turkey Balls (see page 95) with rice and vegetables; Frozen Pineapple Cheesecake Slice (see page 138)

Snacks: Roasted Red Pepper-Almond Dip (see page 69) with vegetable sticks; Lemon-Coconut Macaroons (see page 78)

Day 2

Breakfast: Almond & Apricot Pancakes (see page 30)

Lunch: Peanut Chicken Bites (see page 42), crudités and salad; fresh fruit and nuts

Dinner: Italian Tuna Balls (using gluten-free bread crumbs and flour) (see page 106), vegetables; Peaches with Berry Syrup (see page 128)

Snacks: nuts; Date & Spice Muffins (see page 24)

Day 3

Breakfast: Crunchy Granola Bites (see
page 25) (using gluten-free oats); fruit

Lunch: Tandoori Chicken (see page 44) with
rice cakes, baby corn and sugarsnap peas;
fresh fruit and yogurt

Dinner: Greek Lamb Patties (see page 100)
(using gluten-free bread crumbs), salad;
Summer Berry Ice Cups (see page 125)

Snacks: Almond Linzer Cookies (see
page 75); fresh fruit and seeds

Day 4

Breakfast: Vegetable Rostis with Herby
Cottage Cheese (see page 34)

Lunch: Fruity Salmon Skewers (see page 54),
raw vegetables; Mango Ice Pops
(see page 124)

Dinner: Pork Satay Sticks (see page 98) with
rice and vegetables; Apple & Pecan Tarts
(using gluten-free oats) (see page 139)

Snacks: Chocolate Cupcakes (see page 76);
fresh fruit and nuts

Day 5

Breakfast: Omelet Roll-Ups (see page 38)

Lunch: Tofu & Cashew Burgers (see page 60)
in a gluten-free roll with salad; fresh fruit
and yogurt

Dinner: Cornmeal Fish Cakes (see page 108),
vegetables; Frozen Blueberry & Chocolate
Slice (see page 135)

Snacks: Zucchini & Apple Cake (see page
84); fresh fruit and seeds

vegetarian 5-day menu

Ensuring your child gets sufficient protein, iron, zinc, calcium, magnesium and essential omega-3 fats is particularly important if they are following a vegetarian diet. Include a variety of grains, beans and lentils, eggs and dairy products as well as nuts and seeds to ensure sufficient protein and mineral intake. Focus on a range of vegetables daily, including dark green leafy vegetables such as spinach, broccoli and kale for iron, and accompany with vitamin C-rich foods like fresh fruit to enhance absorption. This menu plan is free from meat, poultry, fish and seafood. Check labels to make sure any cheeses are vegetarian.

Day 1

Breakfast: Cranberry-Seed Bread (see page 22) with nut butter

Lunch: Tofu & Cashew Burgers (see page 60) in a roll with salad; fresh fruit and yogurt

Dinner: Vegetable Samosas (see page 112), spinach and peas; Grilled Pineapple (see page 130)

Snacks: Choc-Nut Lemon Bars (see page 81); Teriyaki Mixed Seeds (see page 86)

Day 2

Breakfast: Tomato Bagel Melts (see page 36)

Lunch: Cheese & Sun-Dried Tomato Polenta Toasts (see page 64) with crudités; Peaches with Berry Syrup (see page 128)

Dinner: Crisp Tofu Skewers (see page 114), rice cakes and broccoli spears; Fruit Slice (see page 136)

Snacks: nuts and fresh fruit; Apricot-Oat Slices (see page 80)

Day 3

Breakfast: Berry Blinis with Sweet Cherry
Sauce (see page 29)

Lunch: Babaganoush with Pita Triangles (see
page 61) with salad; Almond-Chocolate
Butter on Apple Wedges (see page 73)

Dinner: Tapas Soufflé Omelet (see page 118);
Frozen Pineapple Cheesecake Slice (see
page 138)

Snacks: Pumpkin-Seed Buns (see page 85);
fresh fruit and seeds

Day 4

Breakfast: Chocolate Peanut Waffles (see
page 32) with fruit

Lunch: Easy Sushi Rolls (see page 57), rice
cakes; fresh fruit and yogurt

Dinner: Risotto Cheese Balls (see page 111),
corn and carrots; Coconut Squares (see
page 127)

Snacks: fresh fruit with nut butter; Teriyaki
Mixed Seeds (see page 86)

Day 5

Breakfast: Tropical Breakfast Bars
(see page 26)

Lunch: Creamy Dips (see page 69) and
Chunky Breadsticks (see page 87); Fruit
Slice (see page 136)

Dinner: Mini Vegetable Quiches (see page
119) and salad; Summer Berry Ice Cups
(see page 125)

Snacks: yogurt and fruit; nuts or seeds

INDEX

A
Almond & Apricot Pancakes 30
Almond-Chocolate Butter on
    Apple Wedges 73
Almond Linzer Cookies 75
Almond Pizza 117
Apple & Pecan Tarts 139
Apple-Cinnamon French
    Toast 31
Apricot-Oat Slices 80
Asian-Spiced Duck 96
Avocado Bagel Melts 36

B
Babaganoush with Pita Triangles
    61
Baked Ham & Egg Cups 48
Baked Phyllo Rollls 51
Banana Choc-Nut Bites 134
Bean & Cheese Bites 66
Beef & Mushroom Potato Cups
    104
Beet & Beef Mini Burgers 102
Berry Blinis with Sweet Cherry
    Sauce 29

C
Carrot & Cheese Roulade 121
Carrot & Raisin Buns 23
Cheese & Sun-Dried Tomato
    Polenta Toasts 64
Cheesy-Chili Muffins 39
Chicken Turnovers 43
Chicken Kiev Patties 90
Chicken Wings with Chili-
    Tomato Sauce 91
Chicken Yakitori Sticks 45
Choc-Nut Lemon Bars 81
Chocolate Cupcakes 76
Chocolate Peanut Waffles 32
Chunky Breadsticks 87
Coconut Squares 127
Coconut-Salmon Sticks with
    Tomato Chutney 105
Cornmeal Fish Cakes 108
Cranberry-Seed Bread 22
Cranberry Biscotti 74
Creamy Mackerel Tarts 109
Creamy Dips 69
Creamy Trout Pitas 56
Crisp Pork Bites 97

Crisp Drumsticks 92
Crisp Spiced Shrimp 58
Crisp Tofu Skewers 114
Crunchy Granola Bites 25

D
Date & Spice Muffins 24
Duck Lettuce Wraps 46

E
Easy Sushi Rolls 57

F
Fig & Goat Cheese Bruschetta 67
Frozen Blueberry & Chocolate
    Slice 135
Frozen Pineapple Cheesecake
    Slice 138
Fruit Slice 136
Fruity Salmon Skewers 54
Fruity Popovers 33

G
Greek Lamb Patties 100
Grilled Pineapple 130

H
Herby Koftas 99

I
Ice-Cream Sandwiches 126
Italian Tuna Balls 106

L
Lamb-Stuffed Peppers 50
Lemon Cheesecake 133
Lemon-Coconut Macaroons 78
Lima-Bean Burgers 116

M
Mango Ice Pops 124
Mango-Orange Crêpes 131
Meaty Pasta Slice 103
Mediterranean Potato
    Cakes 65
Mexican Corn Fritters 35
Mini Vegetable Quiches 119
Mixed Pepper Tartlets 120

N
No-Bake Whoopie Pies 79

O
Omelet Roll-ups 38

P
Peaches with Berry Syrup 128
Peanut Butter & Coconut Balls 72
Peanut Chicken Bites 42
Pesto & Lamb Frittatas 101
Pigs in Blankets 49
Pomegranate-Glazed Chicken
    Thighs 93
Pork & Apple Burgers 47
Pumpkin-Seed Buns 85
Pork Satay Sticks 98

Q
Quesadilla Wedges 62

R
Raisin-Quinoa Slices 28
Ricotta, Pear & Walnut
    Sandwiches 59
Risotto Cheese Balls 111

S
Shrimp & Tomato Fritters 110
Spicy Chicken Kebabs 94
Squash Scones 82
Steak Gremolata Rolls 52
Stuffed Tomatoes 68
Summer Berry Ice Cups 125
Sweet Cherry Samosas 132
Sweet Potato Falafels 113

T
Tandoori Chicken Strips 44
Tapas Soufflé Omelet 118
Teriyaki Mixed Seeds 86
Thai-Spiced Turkey Balls 95
Tofu & Cashew Burgers 60
Tostada Chili Wedges 53
Tropical Breakfast Bars 26

V
Vegetable Rostis with Herby
    Cottage Cheese 34
Vegetable Samosas 112

Z
Zucchini & Apple Cake 84